Deleuze's Kantian Ethos

Plateaus – New Directions in Deleuze Studies

'It's not a matter of bringing all sorts of things together under a single concept but rather of relating each concept to variables that explain its mutations.'
Gilles Deleuze, *Negotiations*

Series Editors
Ian Buchanan, University of Wollongong
Claire Colebrook, Penn State University

Editorial Advisory Board
Keith Ansell Pearson, Ronald Bogue, Constantin V. Boundas, Rosi Braidotti, Eugene Holland, Gregg Lambert, Dorothea Olkowski, Paul Patton, Daniel Smith, James Williams

Titles available in the series
Christian Kerslake, *Immanence and the Vertigo of Philosophy: From Kant to Deleuze*
Jean-Clet Martin, *Variations: The Philosophy of Gilles Deleuze*, translated by Constantin V. Boundas and Susan Dyrkton
Simone Bignall, *Postcolonial Agency: Critique and Constructivism*
Miguel de Beistegui, *Immanence – Deleuze and Philosophy*
Jean-Jacques Lecercle, *Badiou and Deleuze Read Literature*
Ronald Bogue, *Deleuzian Fabulation and the Scars of History*
Sean Bowden, *The Priority of Events: Deleuze's Logic of Sense*
Craig Lundy, *History and Becoming: Deleuze's Philosophy of Creativity*
Aidan Tynan, *Deleuze's Literary Clinic: Criticism and the Politics of Symptoms*
Thomas Nail, *Returning to Revolution: Deleuze, Guattari and Zapatismo*
François Zourabichvili, *Deleuze: A Philosophy of the Event* with *The Vocabulary of Deleuze* edited by Gregg Lambert and Daniel W. Smith, translated by Kieran Aarons
Frida Beckman, *Between Desire and Pleasure: A Deleuzian Theory of Sexuality*
Nadine Boljkovac, *Untimely Affects: Gilles Deleuze and an Ethics of Cinema*
Daniela Voss, *Conditions of Thought: Deleuze and Transcendental Ideas*
Daniel Barber, *Deleuze and the Naming of God: Post-Secularism and the Future of Immanence*
F. LeRon Shults, *Iconoclastic Theology: Gilles Deleuze and the Secretion of Atheism*
Janae Sholtz, *The Invention of a People: Heidegger and Deleuze on Art and the Political*
Marco Altamirano, *Time, Technology and Environment: An Essay on the Philosophy of Nature*
Sean McQueen, *Deleuze and Baudrillard: From Cyberpunk to Biopunk*
Ridvan Askin, *Narrative and Becoming*
Marc Rölli, *Gilles Deleuze's Transcendental Empiricism: From Tradition to Difference* translated by Peter Hertz-Ohmes
Guillaume Collett, *The Psychoanalysis of Sense: Deleuze and the Lacanian School*
Ryan J. Johnson, *The Deleuze-Lucretius Encounter*
Allan James Thomas, *Deleuze, Cinema and the Thought of the World*
Cheri Lynne Carr, *Deleuze's Kantian Ethos: Critique as a Way of Life*
Alex Tissandier, *Affirming Divergence: Deleuze's Reading of Leibniz*

Forthcoming volumes
Justin Litaker, *Deleuze and Guattari's Political Economy*
Nir Kedem, *A Deleuzian Critique of Queer Thought: Overcoming Sexuality*
Felice Cimatti, *Becoming-animal: Philosophy of Animality After Deleuze*, translated by Fabio Gironi

Visit the Plateaus website at edinburghuniversitypress.com/series/plat

DELEUZE'S KANTIAN ETHOS
Critique as a Way of Life

Cheri Lynne Carr

EDINBURGH
University Press

Edinburgh University Press is one of the leading university presses in the UK. We publish academic books and journals in our selected subject areas across the humanities and social sciences, combining cutting-edge scholarship with high editorial and production values to produce academic works of lasting importance. For more information visit our website: edinburghuniversitypress.com

© Cheri Lynne Carr, 2018

Edinburgh University Press Ltd
The Tun – Holyrood Road
12(2f) Jackson's Entry
Edinburgh EH8 8PJ

Typeset in Sabon by
Servis Filmsetting Ltd, Stockport, Cheshire

A CIP record for this book is available from the British Library

ISBN 978 1 4744 0771 7 (hardback)
ISBN 978 1 4744 0772 4 (webready PDF)
ISBN 978 1 4744 0773 1 (epub)

The right of Cheri Lynne Carr to be identified as the author of this work has been asserted in accordance with the Copyright, Designs and Patents Act 1988, and the Copyright and Related Rights Regulations 2003 (SI No. 2498).

Contents

Acknowledgements	vi
Abbreviations	vii
Introduction: The Problem of a Deleuzian Ethics	1

Part I: Deleuze's Critical Philosophy – Kantian Critique and the Differential Theory of Faculties

1	The Deleuzian Subject	27
2	The Theory of Faculties	50
3	Immanent Critique	80

Part II: Critique as an Ethos – A Handbook for a Way Out

4	Critical Ethos	101
5	Moral Destiny and Culture	120
6	Violence of Critique	138

Conclusion: Ethics and the Richness of the Possible	155
Index	157

Acknowledgements

For the love and steadfastness I needed to bring these thoughts to realisation, I am deeply indebted to Janae Sholtz. Her encouragement, intellectual energy and friendship at every stage of my writing has been irreplaceable. Likewise, many friends and mentors have helped me shape these thoughts over the years, either through their kind commentary, their inspiration, or their material, everyday support: Mary Beth Mader, Len Lawlor, Robert Bernasconi, Sarah Clark Miller, Hoke Robinson, Tom Nenon, Nancy Simco, Deb Tollefsen, Daniel Smith, Marc Djaballah, Joe Hughes, Levi Bryant, Dale Wilkerson, Jeff Bell, Erinn Gilson, Bryan Bannon, David Gougelet, and the entire community of thinkers at the University of Memphis.

Thanks especially to LaGuardia Community College, President Gail Mellow, the City University of New York (CUNY), and the LaGuardia Center for Teaching and Learning for the creation of a mutually supportive community dedicated to critical thinking and practices. I have been privileged to enjoy the intellectual inspiration of my colleagues John Chaffee, Shannon Proctor, Dana Trusso, Jessica Boehman, Richard Brown, Vera Albrecht, Payal Doctor, Emmanuel Nartey, Leslie Aarons, Andrew McFarland and Minerva Ahumada. Thank you for pushing me always to grow. Thanks also to Carol MacDonald for believing in my project, to the Edinburgh University Press staff for assistance in its progression, to Brian Hopper and Tim Clark for their excellent suggestions and attention to detail, and to Ian Buchanan and Claire Colebrook for accepting my project into this series.

My most heartfelt gratitude goes to my family, Alex and Penelope, to my parents Velita and John, and to my siblings Jeannie, Joseph and Danielle – for their unfailing love, encouragement and patience.

Abbreviations

AO	Gilles Deleuze and Félix Guattari, *Anti-Oedipus*, trans. Robert Hurley, Mark Seem and Helen R. Lane, Minneapolis: University of Minnesota Press, 1983.
B	Gilles Deleuze, *Bergsonism*, trans. Hugh Tomlinson and Barbara Habberjam, New York: Zone Books, 1991.
CII	Gilles Deleuze, *Cinema II: The Time-Image*, trans. Hugh Tomlinson and Robert Galeta, Minneapolis: University of Minnesota Press, 1989.
CJ	Immanuel Kant, *Critique of the Power of Judgement*, trans. Paul Guyer and Eric Matthews, New York: Cambridge, 2000.
CPR	Immanuel Kant, *Critique of Pure Reason*, trans. Paul Guyer and Allen W. Wood, New York: Cambridge, 1998.
D	Gilles Deleuze and Claire Parnet, *Dialogues*, trans. Hugh Tomlinson and Barbara Habberjam, New York: Columbia University Press, 2007.
DR	Gilles Deleuze, *Difference and Repetition*, trans. Paul Patton, London: Athlone, 1994.
ES	Gilles Deleuze, *Empiricism and Subjectivity*, trans. Constantin Boundas, New York: Columbia University Press, 1991.
F	Gilles Deleuze, *Foucault*, trans. Seán Hand, Minneapolis: University of Minnesota Press, 1988.
IUH	Immanuel Kant, 'Idea for a Universal History with Cosmopolitan Intent', trans. Allen W. Wood, in *Anthropology, History, and Education*, ed. Günter Zöller and Robert B. Louden, New York: Cambridge University Press, 2007.
KCP	Gilles Deleuze, *Kant's Critical Philosophy*, trans. Hugh Tomlinson and Barbara Habberjam, Minneapolis: University of Minnesota Press, 1984.
N	Gilles Deleuze, *Negotiations*, trans. Martin Joughin, New York: Columbia, 1995.
NP	Gilles Deleuze, *Nietzsche and Philosophy*, trans. Hugh Tomlinson, New York: Columbia, 1986.

PI   Gilles Deleuze, *Pure Immanence: Essays on A Life*, trans. Anne Boyman, New York: Zone Books, 2001.
PS   Gilles Deleuze, *Proust and Signs: The Complete Text*, trans. Richard Howard, Minneapolis: University of Minnesota Press, 2000.
TP   Gilles Deleuze and Félix Guattari, *A Thousand Plateaus*, trans. Brian Massumi, Minneapolis: University of Minnesota Press, 1987.
WE   Michel Foucault, 'What is Enlightenment?', trans. Catherine Porter, in *The Foucault Reader*, ed. Paul Rabinow, New York: Pantheon Books, 1984.
WG   Gilles Deleuze, *What is Grounding?*, trans. Arjen Kleinherenbrink, Grand Rapids: &&& Publishing, 2015.
WP   Gilles Deleuze and Félix Guattari, *What is Philosophy?*, trans. Graham Burchell and Hugh Tomlinson, New York: Columbia University Press, 1994.

To my father, John Thomas Carr, Jr.

Introduction: The Problem of a Deleuzian Ethics

Fascism Within the Self

Fascism has been and continues to be one of our most pressing issues. As an ideology that espouses ultranationalist ideals of superiority to justify authoritarian enforcements of exclusion and conformity, it is a direct and existential threat to freedom. But fascism has taken many faces, and the defeat of Mussolini's Partito Nazionale Fascista (PNF) did not prevent the rise of new forms of fascism decades later.[1] Today, neo- and proto-fascisms continue to emerge in ultranationalist, authoritarian and extremist consolidations of power across the globe.[2] Even in the United States, where fascism has long been dismissed as an historical or exclusively European problem, the recent popular emergence of rhetoric and postures evocative of or even explicitly related to fascist ideology has inspired widespread comparison and a new sense of the real, imminent danger that fascism poses.[3] As Gilles Deleuze and Félix Guattari point out in *Anti-Oedipus*, fascism was not just a 'bad moment' or an 'historical error': fascism has yet to be overcome (AO 29–30). Why this is the case and what we might do about it are the frame in which the project of this book should be understood.

But perhaps the label of fascism is thrown around too easily. Political scientist Sheri Berman argues that attempts to equate 'historical fascism' with global trends toward far-right authoritarian extremism, particularly in the United States, ignore the fact that historical fascism was anti-democratic, suspicious of capitalism, and made a virtue of blind obedience to authority.[4] Berman worries that looseness in the definition of fascism threatens to occlude the real problems, which are exclusionary rather than inclusionary practices. The legitimisation of exclusionary policies such as anti-immigration laws only increases in the wake of the failure of the habits, norms and institutions necessary for democracies to function – not in the wake of anti-capitalist military coup d'états. Moreover, Berman worries that the looseness in the definition deflects attention away from the responsibility that the left carries in contributing to the creation of a state of affairs conducive to a rise in exclusionary practices.[5] However, as Eugene Holland has pointed out, 'the point of revisiting a political concept such as fascism is not to erect a catch-all definition valid for all time, but to reconstruct the concept in relation to an Event – in this case, the advent of twenty-first century fascism in the United States'.[6] The urgency today of returning to Deleuze and Guattari's work on fascism in the 1970s stems from their identification of a deeper form of fascism within the self, of which current neo- and proto-fascist political activity and formations are important indices.

In making the claim that fascism has yet to be overcome, Deleuze and Guattari are returning to a question posed by Marxist psychoanalyst Wilhelm Reich.[7] Reich's work, like Deleuze and Guattari's, begins by identifying 'the fundamental problem of political philosophy' as one of understanding the tendency of people to choose reactionary and authoritarian systems of government even when those systems are not in their own interest (AO 29). Reich wanted to understand how regimes as oppressive and antithetical to democratic ideals as Nazism and Fascism could nevertheless count on millions of ordinary and educated people's fervent support. Why do people – many people, all at once – support systems oppressive to themselves? Why particularly in the early twentieth century? Why suddenly again now? Reich rejected interpretations that attributed the rise of fascism to such causes as the manipulation of State mythologies, the mysterious charisma of individual leaders, or the erosion of liberal European morality under the influence of nihilism (what are now sometimes derisively called 'post-truth' philosophies).[8] Reich saw such explanations as seeking to cast the populace as unwitting dupes of a small group of devoted extremists.[9] But whether extremism is coming from the right or the left, its influence on the decision-making of millions of people might account for a measure of the rise and endurance of fascism, but not all of it. After all, ultranationalist, far-right and authoritarian candidates are regularly democratically voted into office, as Berman points out. Given this, an account of the endurance of fascism would be better served by emphasising not how different 'those people' are from 'us', but what might be at the basis of fascism's allure for us all. Reich's suggestion in this regard is in line with more recent scholarship highlighting the fundamental populism of fascism.[10] As Reich saw it – and this becomes definitive for Deleuze and Guattari – fascism was not a result of mass ignorance or deception; rather, 'at a certain point, under a certain set of conditions, [the people] *wanted* fascism' (AO 29, emphasis in original).

The most significant contribution of Reich's psychoanalytic approach to understanding the endurance of fascism is his diagnosis of its roots within conditions that create a desire for fascism within us. Deleuze and Guattari are not speaking only of the emergence of fascist regimes, but of the fascism that exists at the very basis of our psychic make-up. As such, the goal here is not to engage directly in debates about whether the multiple new forms and harbingers of fascism today are exact replicas of historical fascism – as fascinating as those debates are. Rather, the possibility of the proliferation of multiple forms of neo- and proto-fascism exists because the eradication of the threat of fascism cannot just happen in the context of politics but must happen on the unconscious level of desire. Evans and Reid's Deleuzo-Guattarian definition of fascism as the phenomenon of the desire for one's own repression captures the essence of what is at stake.[11]

There are numerous competing accounts of the conditions sufficient to produce a desire for one's own repression. It is important to distinguish the account Deleuze and Guattari develop from the psychoanalytic ones that nonetheless orient them, such as Reich's, as well as the psychoanalytic accounts that undergird popular conceptions today, such as Julia Kristeva's. According to Reich, the 'perversion' of desire characteristic of fascism emerges from the authoritarian parenting styles of the industrialised world. This authoritarianism in the family produces adults conflicted between a desire for freedom and a fear of the social responsibilities that come with that freedom. However, for Reich, this fear is not a basic drive – it is one to which we have been conditioned. Our authoritarian upbringing has separated us from what we can do: from our capacity for autonomous regulation, from our ability to guide our lives without relying on external 'expertise', and from the material resources necessary for taking chances.[12] Reich traces this phenomenon principally to societies that repress women and adolescents' freedom to fully express their sexuality. Sexual repression perverts our desires, mutating them into the sadistic desires of war, murder, torture, rape and the multiple iterations of exploitation, slavery and scapegoating we continue to struggle to eliminate. Reich's solution to this is the therapeutic encouragement of sexual expression and resistance to authoritarian parenting styles. For Kristeva, on the other hand, the desire for fascism expresses a form of 'defensive hatred' – a reactive approach to the loss of the comforting patriarchal, national and religious myths at the basis, she argues, of the healthy development of the ego.[13] Kristeva's account lines up with prevailing interpretations that attribute the rise of National Socialism in the interwar period of the 1930s to the humiliation and punitive peace treaty imposed upon Germany after the First World War, but it is also sensitive to the ways in which pre-war philosophers and sociologists such as Erich Fromm, Émile Durkheim and Max Weber saw secularisation as stripping us of the foundational stories and myths that gave us identity, meaning and hope.[14] Kristeva's solution involves building new narratives around nationhood that are humanistic, cosmopolitan and inclusive – welcoming otherness rather than rejecting it. She believes that these new nationalist stories will produce healthy individuals who nonetheless welcome otherness. Psychoanalytic accounts like Reich's and Kristeva's that emphasise a fundamental problem of ego or identity formation are powerful narratives, yet they find themselves facing an impasse in relation to fascism, namely, that their very emphasis on individual human identity is inadvertently complicit with the exclusionary orientation and practices of historical, neo- and proto-fascisms.

The political trend, particularly in the United States and Eastern Europe, has been to move from the historical fascism that sought to suppress individuality through the use of strong state discipline in the quest for unity, purity and national supremacy, to forms of neo- and proto-fascism that emphasise individuality while seeking to direct and control the popular narrative through exploitation of new media for the purpose of creating a desire for the 'small-government' deregulation of industry and markets in favour of the continued supremacy of those in positions of extreme wealth and power. In other words, the imposition of direct state 'discipline' has been replaced with a more diffuse, indirect 'control' of the means of education, but with the same corporatist[15] and authoritarian agenda, masked in a cult of individualism.[16] And while it may have appeared as though historical fascism contested individualism by idealising the surrender of individual interests in favour of the party's interests, it nonetheless anticipated a certain brand of individualism in the cultivation of the hero, which Umberto Eco identified as one of the fourteen general properties of fascist thinking.[17] Eco observes that because the 'Ur-Fascist' (or eternal fascist) perspective implies contempt for the weak, 'everybody is educated to become a hero', one who submits his will to that of the party and craves death as a reward for his heroic

Introduction

life. This conception of heroism as normalised martyrdom (as for ISIS and Al Qaeda, but also for reactionary Christian movements like Quiverfull, and arguably for the United States' Republican-backed attempts to block universal healthcare) leads to the embrace of a cult of death in which the hero 'is impatient to die [and] in his impatience, he more frequently sends other people to death'.[18]

There is a relationship of mutual dependence between this ideal of heroic martyrdom and the model of individual, 'atomistic' identity operative in psychoanalysis and largely throughout the Western moral imaginary. As Charles Taylor diagnoses it, the control exerted on people through the education of desire that produces fascism lies partially in the myth of atomism: 'the view of human nature as metaphysically independent from society' and of society as 'constituted by individuals for the fulfillment of ends which were primarily individual'.[19] On the view Taylor develops, the atomistic individual prioritises their own rights over their social obligations.[20] This is one facet of the ideology at the core of neoliberalism. When Isabell Lorey argues that the Western model of the autonomous subject has always required keeping our 'others' in precarity, she is showing how the ideals – whether implicit or explicit – of heroic exceptionality, of destruction as purification, and of the priority of individual rights over community obligations together form a view of the other as dispensable.[21] This is why the phenomenon of fascism (as the desire for one's own repression) is inseparable from the oppression of minorities, from violence against critics, and from a type of nationalism that operates as a racist dog-whistle.[22] Fascism is inseparable from the oppression of others because it is an expression of the desire for repression of one's own multiple, imbricated and fluid selves, as will be expanded on in detail in Chapter 1. This desire is constructed through the everyday practices that echo the myth of the other as competition and of strength as defeat of the competition. This expresses a kind of neoliberal fascism baked into the everyday life and practices within capitalist systems. Individualism is the desire for one's own repression because it is sympathetic to this story of competition; as such it seeks privatisation and the de-investing of the social field because the idea of genuine obligations toward the outside are seen as instances of weakness and illegitimate incursions on the rights of individuals. It relies on an exclusionary difference rather than an inclusive one – a repetition of the same rather than a repetition of difference – that considers exclusion a form of strength.

What this indicates is that psychoanalytic anti-fascist interventions are treating the mutating symptoms of fascism without attending to the underlying cause: these mutating versions of mythic individualism and competition. While many psychoanalysts who focus on the Oedipalised family and the strengthening of a healthy ego strongly reject the racist, xenophobic, misogynistic and authoritarian features of neo-fascist thinking, psychoanalysis itself does not fully contest neo-fascism at its foundation because it shares the same investment in individualistic identity. In contrast, as Jeff Bell has pointed out, while Deleuze would agree with theorists like Robert Nozick[23] that 'there is no social entity that transcends the desires, interests, and freedoms of individuals', he and Guattari would also argue that there are no 'individuals as transcendent predetermining unities. Both individual entities and social entities are created, or they are assemblages (i.e., assemblages of molar and molecular segments)'.[24] Janae Sholtz analyses a similar impasse in one of our major areas of contemporary progressive political thought. She writes that when thought 'still takes identity as its standard and thus begins from the products of social determinates rather than the investments of desire that produce them', the effect is an impasse that nullifies deep transformation.[25] Sholtz's suggestion of an 'intersectional transversality' as a way of taking up and pushing further Kimberlé Crenshaw's pivotal intersectional analysis is illustrative of the Deleuzo-Guattarian approach to psychoanalysis: to take it up and push it further is to contest identity, to open it up to the possibilities of singular, non-localisable, creative relations of becoming.

So, Reich's shift to emphasise desire's positivity – to ask the question of why we desire fascism when it denies us political and actual power – is the right direction, and Deleuze and Guattari seek to take this question further.[26] For them, desire is not a desire for power; it is a power. It is the positive operation of the unconscious and thus precedes the ego or its even tacit interests: 'Production as process overtakes all idealistic categories and constitutes a cycle whose relationship to desire is that of an immanent principle' (AO 5). Desire is socially constructed, it is an assemblage, and fascism produces desires which desire their own repression. In this light the focus on the Oedipal family and strong individuation in a healthy ego does not go far enough because of its too narrow focus on the construct rather than on the mythic and educational paradigms that formed the investments of desire that formed the construct. In analysing the formation of desire, Deleuze and Guattari's account of fascism attends to different moments in the move from the first to the

Introduction

second volume of *Capitalism and Schizophrenia*.[27] In *Anti-Oedipus*, fascism is a freezing or fixation of desire,[28] while in *A Thousand Plateaus* fascism will appear as 'a kind of acceleration of desire or energy'.[29] These analyses work together to form a picture of fascism as a constant danger (because it is a part) within the productive cycle of desire itself. For production to 'continue' there must be stops or breaks in the flow of desire, in order to create a 'space' for new production. What attracts desire is *'the degree of development of productive forces'*; that is, desire's own empowerment through the development of its productive forces, which Eugene Holland points to as 'a crucial factor in explaining the primal populism of historical fascism'.[30] However, even though desire does not seek any particular social representations or libidinal investments, when 'social representations impose both a form and a set of more or less fixed images on desire . . . The more fixed the images are, the greater is the degree of paranoia and fascistic tendencies characterizing that desire'.[31] For Deleuze and Guattari, we choose fascism because it augments our feeling of power – power over ourselves (to control the incessant production of desire) and power over others. But this desire necessarily becomes suicidal: 'Unlike the totalitarian State, which does its utmost to seal all possible lines of flight, fascism is constructed on an intense line of flight, which it transforms into a line of pure destruction and abolition' (TP 230).[32] It becomes suicidal because, once desire becomes fixed on a static, molar social representation and arrangement of power, its incessant production must turn inward, like a feverish anxiety. Because its production depends on cessation (in the idealised heroic individual), this anxiety translates as an eagerness to destroy itself in its cathexis with the molar (or molarised) representation it has fixed upon, as lived through its 'molecular' family, communities, schools, etc. Idealistic self-immolation as consistency of virtue: this is the danger of suicide within violent daily regime/habit change (TP 161). And in its eagerness to destroy itself, it more easily destroys others. Eco's 'everybody is educated to become a hero' can be expressed in Deleuzo-Guattarian terms with the idea that desire is 'educated' or assembled into a heroic martyrdom or war machine with no other object than war.

As Foucault put it in his preface to *Anti-Oedipus*: 'the major enemy . . . is fascism. And not only historical fascism . . . but also the fascism within us all, in our heads, and in our everyday behaviour, the fascism that causes us to love power, to desire the very thing that dominates and exploits us' (AO xiii). What Deleuze and Guattari are pointing to is the hidden fascism that seeps into the everyday: the fascism within the self. This is the deeper form of fascism that makes possible the phenomenon of millions of educated people – us – wanting authoritarian and exclusionary neo-fascism today. Whereas totalitarianism produces conformity through pressure from above and without, fascism produces conformity and oppression through the everyday – the 'molecular' family, community, schools, etc. What we must be vigilant about are the ways in which we reaffirm and reinvest the repressive power of the State in our most intimate relationships, habits and negotiations of daily, mundane power (the micropolitics of everyday practices). Totalitarianism acts from without but fascism infects the veins of daily life. It develops within us as 'a cancerous body' of 'microformations already shaping postures, attitudes, perceptions, expectations, semiotic systems, etc.' (TP 214). This is why Brad Evans and Julian Reid begin their excellent volume on *Deleuze and Fascism* by emphasising that 'the problem of fascism today cannot simply be addressed as that of the potential or variable return and reconstitution of fascism, as if fascism had ever, or could ever, "disappear", only to return and be made again, like some spectral figure from the past'.[33] It is not an historically constituted regime, but a 'diffuse' 'micro-fascism' of the everyday. What this means is that fascism is not going to go away by getting rid of individualism and identity: that this is only partly a theoretical or political question. Fascism infects the everyday. It is as diffuse as power. For Evans and Reid, politics necessitates desire as desire for power and they consider it axiomatic to acknowledge that, 'for a life to be lived freely, it cannot fully exorcise the impulse towards or desire for power'.[34] So, the problems of fascism and racism will not be solved by getting rid of identity politics, which has become one of the most powerful vehicles for instigating open discussion of racism and sexism. As a response to white supremacy (what white men just call 'politics'), identity politics has created a counter-narrative for the goal of resistance and empowerment of people of colour. But in truth, all politics is identity politics – which is why there is an urgent need for something different, something like an ethics.

Ethics asks 'How should we live?' and 'What should we do?' at the level of the everyday. It has only been in recent years that readings of Deleuze emphasising the practical dimension of his story no longer seem out of place. The suggestion that there was a practical dimension to Deleuze's thought seemed wrong-headed to many scholars in so far as Deleuze's work, like that of many French philosophers

Introduction

in the 1960s and beyond, resisted traditional principle-based ethical theories. However, that understanding is predicated on a limited conception of ethics. Rather than think of ethics in the sense of a theory that grounds a set of rules in a conception of the Good or a theory of human nature, there is a strong tradition of understanding ethics in terms of an ethos or way of life that expresses a practical attitude that derives from ontology. This way of understanding ethics has its roots in the earliest works of philosophy and has continued through the last century in Foucault's work as well as in that of Pierre Hadot, Alasdair MacIntyre, Charles Taylor, Martha Nussbaum and Martin Heidegger, among others. Deleuze's way of reading ontology is consistent with the tradition of those who believe that ontology must be understood as a discursive practice concerned with modes of being rather than a pure metaphysics of substance. Indeed, a careful reading of the critical trajectory within Deleuze's thought suggests that ontology would be impossible without an actual practical attitude that is not a theory but a choice about oneself that transforms the ways in which one lives in the world.[35] In his last published work, *Pure Immanence: Essays on A Life*, Deleuze wrote that what has been forgotten 'is the unity of life and thought. It is a complex unity: one step for life, one step for thought. Modes of life inspire ways of thinking; modes of thinking create ways of living. Life *activates* thought, and thought *affirms* life' (PI 66). If the productive cycle of desire is a process of identity and group formation – what kind of formations should we love? Is there a real potential to oppose exclusionary collective identities with radically inclusive ones? Is there room for better forms of 'identity' that resist the static cathexis into the heroic, fascistic individual martyr? For forms of community that give us a sense of belonging, purpose and support without devolving into tribalism? As Kristeva suggested, the question of how to resist fascism becomes a question of the evaluation of identities and groups and of the mythic narratives that form those identities and groups. Yet since the problem of fascism is not that some other people are ignorant – rather that it is *our* desire for and love of power that has become fixed and, ultimately, suicidal – we must look to ourselves, to our lives and practices, and to the possibility of carefully dismantling the individual to free not only our creativity but the habituality of those of our practices that limit and oppress others. The question of how to resist fascism therefore becomes the question of evaluating our ethos: what mode of living and thinking will mutually reaffirm freedom? How can we cultivate our desire for freedom rather than our desire for our own repression? And can we take this desire and use it to cultivate systems and institutions that support the freedom of others? This is a dramatically different approach to ethics than those that would ground a set of rules in a conception of the Good or a theory of human nature. It is an anti-fascist ethos radically tied to a Deleuzian theory of how thinking works.

The Search for a Starting Point

Where should we start? Deleuze begins the third chapter of *Difference and Repetition*, titled 'The Image of Thought', with a meditation on the problem of beginning in philosophy. The problem is that 'beginning means eliminating all presuppositions', but in philosophy presuppositions can be both objective and subjective (DR 129). While objective presuppositions are explicitly linked to concepts and thus easily eliminated, subjective presuppositions are implicit in our thinking and therefore more difficult to eliminate. They are more tenacious than objective presuppositions because they appear intuitive. Their origin lies in the implicit – and unconscious – assumption that there are things so fundamental to experience that they are universally understood and therefore beyond both justification and question. Deleuze's example is Descartes' subjective presupposition that everyone knows 'independently of concepts, what is meant by self, thinking, and being' (DR 129).[36]

In everyday experience, these 'implicit biases' or subjective presuppositions operate as 'lenses' that inflect the way we experience the world without us necessarily being aware of them.[37] The idea of 'implicit biases' has become a key concept in debates about race and sex in the United States, as a way of talking about the endurance of institutionalised racism and misogyny within the self – particularly the selves of those who create and sustain racist and misogynistic institutions.[38] These biases are habits of thought formed by our culture, our institutions and our experiences. And they affect everyone. Psychological experiments show that even people who expressly deny believing the racist association of black people with apes 'nonetheless unintentionally affiliate black people with apes'.[39] While it is crucial to call out intentional and conscious forms of racism, misogyny and neo-fascism, these intentional and conscious forms are supported by unconsciously adopted patterns of white supremacist, patriarchal micro-fascism.[40] Consider, for example, the definition of patriarchy suggested by bell hooks. Patriarchy is a 'social disease assaulting

Introduction

the male body' that insists 'males are inherently dominating ... and endowed with the right to dominate' anyone perceived as weak (women, minorities, children, animals, the earth).[41] Patriarchy is a system of values that goes uncritically repeated from one generation to the next yet causes a destruction of relationships that is historically almost never attributed to it directly. Patriarchal thinking is hidden in the ways we speak, relate, think and value. Yet those who repeat patriarchal thinking do not necessarily identify in themselves the values of patriarchy or the mode of fascism. This helps to explain the presence of a not-insignificant number of women in white nationalist groups and the phenomenon of women voting against their own reproductive freedoms.

The confrontation with implicit biases can be a difficult process – perhaps even an 'encounter' in Deleuze's sense. An analysis of your own implicit biases forces you come face to face with the fact that you may not be the person you thought you were – to appreciate the degree to which, as Nietzsche famously put it, 'we are strangers to ourselves'.[42] This is why, for Deleuze and Guattari, resistance to fascism must start from within: 'it is too easy to be antifascist on the molar level, and not even see the fascist inside you, the fascist you yourself sustain and nourish and cherish with molecules both personal and collective' (TP 214–15).[43] Resistance requires a turn inward that goes beyond treating the symptoms to begin addressing the disease, namely the conditions that create the desire for one's own repression, or the exclusionary, atomistic patterns of identity and community formation that encourage the perpetuation of historical fascism in new forms. Where this leads us, perhaps paradoxically, is to Deleuze's encounter with Immanuel Kant.

Deleuze does not think that the problem of subjective presuppositions or implicit biases is limited to a few philosophers here and there. He believes that it is pervasive in the history of philosophy. So, his starting point is a critique of the deepest of these presuppositions, which he identifies as the 'dogmatic Image of thought'. The dogmatic Image of thought is a tacit and unquestioned assumption that recognition or representational thinking is coextensive with what it means to think. However, when the process of recognition is taken as the model for all thinking the results are genuinely harmful. Though recognition is indeed a real and important feature of everyday epistemic relations, by taking it as the model for all thought, the dogmatic Image sets the standard of thinking far too low.[44] Deleuze wants to reserve the term 'thinking' for a process that is more complex, more challenging – and more dangerous – than simple recognition. Moreover, the dogmatic Image of thought makes an empirical claim about thinking but hides the contingency of that claim by asserting that it holds in principle. This is one of the strategies philosophers use to conceal, even from themselves, their biases and presuppositions. As James Williams elegantly summarises it: this 'false step into the transcendent, supposedly empty, form gives the impression of avoiding contingent empirical content whilst still carrying it through'.[45] Finally, recognition tacitly presupposes a form of identity determined from the outside, which ultimately predetermines what can count as thought.[46] As a result, under the dogmatic Image, thought can only compare the new to what is already known – and so it can never move beyond anything but the recognisable (DR 134). Any thought that cannot be reduced to what is recognisable and knowable is dismissed as nonsense, as absurd, or as meaningless. For Deleuze, the practical implication of uncritically accepting the dogmatic Image is that when thought must conform to the necessities of the genesis of knowledge it loses its creative freedom and transformative power. But even more practically, when thinking operates as a means of assigning legitimacy based on a comparison with what is already known, anything perceived as too foreign will be automatically disqualified. This way of thinking of thought lies at the basis of the exclusionary and exploitative practices to which imperialists and fascists subjected the rest of the world for centuries. Indeed, to say that atomistic individualism operates as a 'dogmatic Image of subjects' may be the correct diagnosis. So, the claim that recognition is thinking at its most natural and universal is not a harmless observation but a strategic interpretation with an ulterior teleological motive – the conservativeness of which diminishes and enslaves thought, enslaves us as thinkers, and enslaves others who are perceived as unrecognisable, that is, as those whose perspective and experience of the world does not match the way we have been habituated to seeing it.

The fundamental ethical imperative in Deleuze's early work is to find a way for thought to think difference rather than repeat the same. For Deleuze, 'real' thought – thought freed from the constraints of the dogmatic Image – would be 'unrecognizable' in so far as it contains a power of newness that 'remains forever new' by 'beginning and beginning again' (DR 136). So, even though Deleuze's goal is to be free of the dogmatic Image that determines thought to conform with established norms, he has no hope of achieving this goal if he merely trades one Image of thought for another. This is why he is

Introduction

so insistent that his work is not intended to develop a rival Image of thought, but to discover what he calls 'a thought without Image' (DR 132). Only a thought free from any Image would be free from presuppositions and concealed conformity. Deleuze concludes that real and unrecognisable thought – thought without Image – 'must seek its models among stranger and more compromising adventures' than those of recognition (DR 135).

The model Deleuze turns to for the creation of a thought without Image is Kant's discovery of 'the prodigious domain of the transcendental' (DR 135). Traditionally, Kant's transcendental is understood as the level of conditions of experience. Deleuze initially follows this tradition, but emphasises the importance of a theory of faculties and their genesis for any examination of the transcendental (this will be analysed in detail in Chapter 2).[47] For Kant, what subjects experience is determined by what they can experience, that is, by their capacities or powers. Kant calls these powers or capacities 'faculties'. Faculties are thus not actual experience, but the conditions of experience. As conditions of experience, Kant believes that faculties straddle the line between transcendent objects and subjects' inner experience of those objects. This line between – the transcendental – is the level that Kant believes makes the relation between transcendent objects and subjects' inner experience of those objects possible. In this way Kant transforms the problem of the relationship between subjects and objects into a problem of the relation between faculties. Faculties are thus the content of the transcendental domain, and since Kant discovers the domain of the transcendental through his use of critique, they are the proper objects of critical examination. Kantian critique, which will be treated in detail in Chapter 3, becomes for Deleuze the implicit foundation of all his ethical work. Kant's critique can be distinguished from other forms of critique (such as Descartes' or Hume's sceptical versions) in so far as it is not fundamentally negative.[48] Rather, Kantian critique examines the structure and limitations of the faculty of Reason so as to distinguish and synthesise conflicting perspectives at the deeper level marked out by that examination: the level of the transcendental. Critique is the practice of evaluating what a body can do. As Inna Semetsky puts it, 'Thinking requires turning upon its own *implicit* assumptions so as to be able to express them explicitly: this is a self-reflective, critical element in Deleuze's philosophy.'[49] It reveals our fascisms while offering ways to resist it. The main features of this critical ethics include self-evaluation, open-mindedness, creativity and the realisation of conditions immanent to becoming. Indeed, for Deleuze, ethics is fundamentally concerned with the determination of the critical as the origin of the individuating motives for one's actions. Critique, understood as the determination of the transcendental conditions of modes of being that constitute 'the conditions of real experience', is a necessary element in the genesis of real thinking freed from its constituting forces in so far as self-critique questions and evaluates that by which the given is given (B 23).

The approach to ethics implicit in Deleuze's work is based on the formation of character – a critical character – in much the same way that virtue ethics is. However, unlike Aristotle's virtue ethics, which defines the virtues by reference to a teleological reading of human function, the Deleuzian ethos is based on a radicalised form of Kantian critical practice. Though Deleuze believed that Kant did not pursue his critique far enough, he nonetheless takes what he describes as an 'immanent' Kantian critique as a starting point. What is so evocative for Deleuze about Kant's critique – and that never leaves his use of it throughout its various instantiations in his work – is the idea of a positive evaluation that supposes not that the faculties err, but that they are subject to illusions that critique can help dispel. The Deleuzo-Guattarian schizoanalysis of desire as a positive assemblage of power is thus anticipated in Deleuze's immanent critique of the powers and limits of the faculties. Deleuze's theory of faculties in *Difference and Repetition* can be read as an attempt to produce a 'thought without Image' by applying his immanent version of Kantian critique to the faculties' experience of encounter. This is significant for Deleuze for a number of reasons, one of which is the irony of using Kant's failed critique as a way to stage a 'real' critique of our (and Kant's) subjective presuppositions. This irony is indicative of why analysing Deleuze's reading of Kant is so crucial for articulating his ethos: by radicalising critique he is performing the analysis of Kant's own implicit biases as a way to move 'past' them. But, as Kant himself acknowledged, critique is a never-ending process. The illusions of reason and implicit biases can be analysed and dispelled, but those illusions and biases will form again and again. As Evans and Reid insist, fascism will never go away. As such, the critical ethos that develops in Deleuze's relationship to Kant (discussed in detail in Chapter 4) is one of self-evaluative vigilance regarding the illusions of individualism. Deleuze and Guattari's position is well described by Erinn Gilson as a becoming that 'is always a matter of relation and connection with otherness'. It is, thus, in a sense, always 'intersubjective'. Such intersubjective assemblages are oriented toward creating new ways of living.[50] But even when we live the critical ethos, the fascism within the self is a constant danger because the fixation of desire on a particular social representation or the spiralling of desire toward suicide are part of the productive cycle of desire itself.

By thinking through the orientation toward the self of critique, combined with an understanding of the self as an assemblage, Deleuze's ethos calls for new habits and institutions to support the deterritorialising of sedimented ways of thinking and behaving. The parallel, described in detail in Chapter 5, between Deleuze and Kant's understanding of the problem of culture as a problem of preparing human minds for the experience of the sublime (or the encounter) and, ultimately, for the attainment of morality and freedom, requires an analysis of the potential fascism at the heart of Deleuze's own thinking about education. 'Culture', or '*paideia*', which Deleuze conceives as a 'violent training' at the unconscious level of the faculties that facilitates the movement of each faculty from its empirical to its transcendental exercise, might seem to be problematically fascistic. However, as is developed in Chapter 6, for Deleuze 'culture' prepares the unconscious mind to perceive encounters and Ideas through its idealisation of a constant questioning, exploring and problematising (DR 165). What Deleuze is developing here is a new theory of education as a preliminary training of the affects, a training of the soul for thinking, questioning and transforming through self-critique, or what Braidotti identifies as 'the conditions that are most conducive to cultivating and sustaining the desire for change and in-depth transformation of the dominant, unitary vision of human subjectivity'.[51]

In the Conclusion, this educational practice as critical ethos will be expanded to consider the possibilities for renewed educative practices of de-individuation as a becoming-autonomous. Here, the practice of pedagogy is ethical – in the sense understood by Deleuze when he distinguishes between ethics and morality: while morality is a set of 'constraining' rules for judging actions in their relation to transcendent values, 'ethics' is a set of 'facilitative' (*facultative*) rules that evaluate actions, words and beliefs according to 'the immanent mode of existence' they imply.[52] This is in contrast to the way the distinction is typically understood, where morality is taken to place emphasis on the moral life and ethics on the good life. The interpretation of modes of existence is what Deleuze calls very early on in his work the 'method of dramatization', where 'actions and propositions are interpreted as so many sets of symptoms that express or dramatise the mode of existence of the speaker'.[53] Deleuze seeks within pedagogical practice an 'ethics without morality' that aims at transcending or overcoming one's mode of habitual belief and implicit bias so as to make possible a new mode of self-becoming-other through negotiations across differences and the capacity of becoming affected by experiences foreign to one's own. In general, since modes of existence can be evaluated immanently according to their power or capacity – 'by the manner in which [a mode] actively deploys its power by going to the limit of what it can do'[54] – the ethical task is to intensify or elevate that power but in such a way as to avoid becoming suicidal. Alternatively, as Joe Barker has argued, dramatisation can be understood not as 'dramatising' the mode of existence of a subject (as Dan Smith argues) but as 'the creation of a viewpoint upon the world'. The ethical significance of dramatisation then lies not in its capacity to evaluate modes of existence but in its ability to 'produce ways of unfolding the world in which we do not "imprison" others and in which multiple perspectives are allowed to unfold'.[55]

Both conceptions of dramatisation seem compatible with the way Deleuze presents this immanent conception of ethics not 'as a rejection of Kantianism but, on the contrary, as its *fulfillment*'.[56] But importantly, this ethics does not entail the imposition of a constraining set of values onto others. It is not the authoritarianism of fascistic thinking. On the contrary, what it supports is the possibility of achieving integrity and authenticity within our fluid and imbricated selves by opening up to sharing 'the life-worlds of others'.[57] This is a critical mode of existence that challenges us, makes our lives dangerous, and sweeps us up into an adventure that will turn us into different people whose fight against fascism springs from a 'spirit of ebullient affirmation'.[58]

Notes

1. There is a lively and contentious debate about the definition of fascism, its evolution and multiplication into forms of neo- and post-fascism, and whether individual instances of right-wing populist nationalism should be categorised as fascism at all. See, for example: James A. Gregor, *Interpretations of Fascism*, New York: Routledge, 1997; Robert Paxton, *The Anatomy of Fascism*, New York: Knopf, 2004; and Roger Griffin, *Fascism*, Oxford: Oxford University Press, 1995.
2. A non-exhaustive list of examples could include Vladimir Putin's

Introduction

Russia, Recep Erdoğan's Turkey, the anti-immigrant and anti-media policies of Viktor Orbán's Hungary, Poland's ultra-nationalist and far-right Law and Justice Party; Narendra Modi's India, Abe's nationalist push in Japan, and Rodrigo Duterte's Philippines.

3. Though US President Donald Trump arguably does not fall under Roger Griffin's widely accepted definition of fascism as 'a palingenetic form of populist ultra-nationalism' ('The Palingenetic Core of Generic Fascist Ideology', in A. Campi (ed.), *Che cos'è il fascismo? Interpretazioni e prospecttive di richerche*, Rome: Ideazione editrice, 2003, pp. 97–122), his campaign slogan 'Make America Great Again' evokes the rhetoric of rebirth and nationalism central to Mussolini's appeal, and his policies are explicitly exclusionary and increasingly corporatist. See Robert Kagan's recent opinion in *Forbes*, 'Yes, A Trump Presidency Would Bring Fascism to America', at https://www.forbes.com/sites/realspin/2016/05/31/yes-a-trump-presidency-would-bring-fascism-to-america/#1d17df39526b (last accessed 27 September 2017); and Peter Baker's *New York Times* article, 'Rise of Donald Trump Tracks Growing Debate Over Global Fascism', at https://www.nytimes.com/2016/05/29/world/europe/rise-of-donald-trump-tracks-growing-debate-over-global-fascism.html?mcubz=3&_r=0&GLS=1504206234%7C9EtGX84ZoKFQ1tQZH3bt%2FXuu0PFgTHiCuQM0R%2BGN91k%3D (last accessed 27 September 2017). A recent series of opinion pieces from historians S. Berman, D. Matthews and J. Heer provide the major touchstones and arguments in the debate about whether these governments are fascist in the historical sense. See https://www.washingtonpost.com/opinions/this-is-how-fascism-comes-to-america/2016/05/17/c4e32c58-1c47-11e6-8c7b-6931e66333e7_story.html?utm_term=.84f95ffc35ad (last accessed 27 September 2017).
4. Berman's piece, 'Donald Trump Isn't a Fascism' is available at https://www.vox.com/the-big-idea/2017/1/3/14154300/fascist-populist-trump-democracy (last accessed 27 September 2017).
5. Berman is referring here to a strain of the radical left which idealises Soviet-era socialist authoritarianism, one indicator of which came in 2016 when the Green Party candidate Jill Stein defended Russia's annexation of Crimea.
6. Eugene Holland, 'Schizoanalysis, Nomadology, Fascism', in *Deleuze and Politics*, ed. Ian Buchanan and Nicholas Thoburn, Edinburgh: Edinburgh University Press, 2008, p. 74.
7. Originally published in 1933, Reich significantly revised his major work *The Mass Psychology of Fascism* for the third edition, which was published in 1942. It is to this later edition, on which the 1970 English translation by V. Carfagno is based, that Deleuze and Guattari refer.
8. Roger Griffin, *The Nature of Fascism*, New York: Routledge, 1993. Reich would have similarly rejected Francis Fukuyama's explanation

of the rise of fascism in terms of the human need to find self-worth through identification with a community. See his *The End of History and the Last Man*, Harmondsworth: Penguin, 1992, chapter 31. For an account of the relationship of nihilism to the rise of fascism contemporary with Reich's contrasting view, see B. Croce, 'Il fascismo come pericolo mondiale', in *Per la nuova vita dell'Italia*, Rome: Ricciardi, 1944.

9. See Theodor Adorno, 'Freudian Theory and the Pattern of Fascist Propaganda', in *The Essential Frankfurt School Reader*, ed. A. Arato and E. Gebhardt, New York: Continuum, 2007. Adorno describes the theory of a 'psychology of the masses', coined by Gustave Le Bon, who claims that the masses are de-individualised, irrational, easily influenced, prone to violent action and regressive.

10. See Roger Griffin's *The Nature of Fascism* and his *International Fascism*, London: Bloomsbury, 1998; Stanley G. Payne, *A History of Fascism, 1914–1945*, Madison: University of Wisconsin Press, 1995; and Roger Eatwell, *Fascism: A History*, New York: Penguin, 1996.

11. Brad Evans and Julian Reid (eds), *Deleuze and Fascism*, Abingdon: Routledge, 2013, p. 2. From here on, I will be using Evans and Reid's definition when I refer to 'fascism' while reserving the term 'historical fascism' for the Italian and Nazi fascisms of the 1920s to 1940s and the terms 'neo-fascism' and 'proto-fascism' to refer to the various forms of fascist-adjacent, far-right ultranationalist, racist, patriarchal and authoritarian political extremisms that have arisen since the defeat of Mussolini and Hitler.

12. Reich believed that this fear of social responsibility was particularly prevalent among people with some but precarious resources because they enjoy a measure of economic stability that is nonetheless fragile.

13. See Julia Kristeva, *Nations without Nationalism*, New York: Columbia University Press, 1993.

14. See Emilio Gentile, 'Fascism as Political Religion', *Journal of Contemporary History* 25:2/3 (1990), pp. 229–51; and Payne, *A History of Fascism*.

15. See Dave Renton, *Fascism: Theory and Practice*, London: Pluto Press, 1999, for a nuanced analysis of Italian fascism that shows that fascism's anti-capitalism was more rhetorical than actual. The fascists in fact shored up the commercial banks, kept open the department stores, and left intact the Confederation of Industry. Renton includes an excellent account of Mussolini's report to the Senate in 1934 in which he claimed that private property completes the human personality.

16. See Michel Foucault, 'Governmentality', trans. Rosi Braidotti and revised by Colin Gordon, in Graham Burchell, Colin Gordon and Peter Miller (eds), *The Foucault Effect: Studies in Governmentality*, Chicago:

Introduction

University of Chicago Press, 1991, pp. 87–104, and Gilles Deleuze, 'Postscript on the Societies of Control', *October* 59 (1992), pp. 3–7.

17. Umberto Eco, 'Ur-Fascism', *New York Review of Books*, 22 June 1995, at http://www.nybooks.com/articles/1995/06/22/ur-fascism (last accessed 28 September 2017).
18. Ibid. In *A Thousand Plateaus*, Deleuze and Guattari cite a remark by Paul Virilio for their understanding of fascism as a 'suicidal State', a war machine that reverses the line of flight into a line of destruction (TP 230–1).
19. Charles Taylor, 'Atomism', in *Philosophy and the Human Sciences: Philosophical Papers, Vol. 2*, Cambridge: Cambridge University Press, 1985, p. 189.
20. In contrast, Taylor argues 'not just that men cannot physically survive alone, but much more that they only develop their characteristically human capacities in society' (Ibid. p. 188).
21. See Isabell Lorey, *State of Insecurity: Government of the Precarious*, London: Verso, 2015. See also Ewa Majewska, 'Weak Resistance in Feminist Protests' (2017), at https://www.ica.art/whats-on/ewa-majewska-weak-resistance-feminist-protests (last accessed 28 September 2017).
22. Indeed, tying the definition of fascism to nationalism may underplay its racism. Cf. James Gregor's argument that 'Nazi Germany violated democratic notions of civil rights and the political autonomy of other nation-states not because it was "ultranationalistic", but because it was *racist*, and, if anything, *ultraracist*' (*Interpretations of Fascism*, xx).
23. This is in reference to Robert Nozick's work in the 1970s, particularly *Anarchy, State, and Utopia* (New York: Basic Books, 1974), which, though he later largely repudiated its individualism, remains foundational for libertarianism.
24. Jeffrey A. Bell, 'Between Individualism and Socialism: Deleuze's Micropolitics of Desire', paper presented to the Association for Political Theory, Calvin College, Grand Rapids, 17 October 2003, p. 15. Available at https://www2.southeastern.edu/Academics/Faculty/jbell/micropolitics.pdf (last accessed 7 September 2017).
25. See Janae Sholtz, 'Schizoanalysis and the Deterritorialisations of Transnational Feminisms', in *Deleuze and the Schizoanalysis of Feminism: Alliances and Allies*, New York: Bloomsbury, 2018.
26. For an excellent comparison of Deleuze and Guattari vis-à-vis Reich, see Holland, 'Schizoanalysis, Nomadology, Fascism'.
27. Ibid. p. 75.
28. John Protevi, 'A Problem of Pure Matter: Fascist Nihilism in *A Thousand Plateaus*', in *Nihilism Now! Monsters of Energy*, ed. Keith Ansell-Pearson and D. Morgan, London: Macmillan, 2000, p. 168.

29. Holland, 'Schizoanalysis, Nomadology, Fascism', p. 75.
30. Ibid. p. 76.
31. Ibid. p. 75.
32. Here Deleuze and Guattari refer to Paul Virilio's distinction between the 'totalitarian state' and the 'suicidal state' of fascism (TP 230).
33. Evans and Reid (eds), *Deleuze and Fascism*, p. 1.
34. Ibid. They go even further when they write that 'Politics demands of us that we not only desire but love power. Such a love cannot be acclaimed non-fascistically' (p. 4).
35. See Anders Raastrup Kristensen, 'Thinking Normativity in Deleuze's Philosophy', *Revisiting Normativity with Deleuze*, ed. Rosi Braidotti and Patricia Pisters, New York: Bloomsbury, 2012, pp. 11–24. 'For Deleuze, the justification of thought as a principle of knowledge is not something outside of thought itself but is an ethics in which thought can be creative. In this sense, the foundation of Deleuze's thinking will always be normativity or ethics' (p. 19).
36. Deleuze contends that this is evidenced in Descartes' decision to define man as a 'thinking thing' rather than as a rational animal. For Descartes, 'rational animal' assumes familiarity with the notions of both rationality and animality whereas 'thinking thing' assumes no previous knowledge of the world but is self-evident to those who think. So, by defining man as a thinking thing, Descartes believes he has eluded the difficulty of presuppositions since, in so far as we all think, 'everyone knows' what it means to think. Deleuze's point is that while Descartes has indeed eluded the objective presuppositions, he has not eluded the subjective ones (DR 129).
37. See John Chaffee's analysis of 'conceptual lenses' in his foundational text *Thinking Critically*, 12th edn, Boston: Cengage, 2018.
38. In the first presidential debate, Lester Holt asked Hillary Clinton to expand on her prior remarks regarding police violence: 'Do you believe that police are implicitly biased against black people?' Clinton replied, 'implicit bias is a problem for everyone, not just police'. There is vibrant scholarly debate about the relationship between memory, perception, socialisation, stigmatisation and history that is helping to shape current debates about prejudice, racism and anti-black violence.
39. Chernoah Sesay Jr., 'Implicit Bias and American History' (2016), at http://www.aaihs.org/implicit-bias-and-american-history (last accessed 18 September 2017). Sesay is referring to Jennifer Eberhardt and Aneeta Rattan's 'The Role of Social Meaning in Inattentional Blindness: When the Gorillas in Our Midst Do *Not* Go Unseen', *Journal of Experimental Social Psychology* 46:6 (2010).
40. The idea of 'implicit biases' shares a connection with Hannah Arendt's analysis of the 'banality of evil' in her 1963 book *Eichmann in Jerusalem*, New York: Penguin Classics, 2006. Evil is banal when it is committed

Introduction

not by fanatics perpetrating exceptional acts but by ordinary people going about their daily lives.
41. bell hooks, 'Understanding Patriarchy' (2012), at http://imagine-noborders.org/pdf/zines/UnderstandingPatriarchy.pdf (last accessed 28 September 2017).
42. In the first section of the Preface to Friedrich Nietzsche, *On the Genealogy of Morals*, Oxford: Oxford Classics, 2009.
43. One of the popular debates in 2017 surrounded the moral status of the 'Antifa' movement of anti-fascist radicals who are willing to deploy violence, intimidation and silencing techniques to resist neo-fascist activities and hate speech. Those who criticise Antifa claim that it hides its own fascism in anti-fascism, contributing to the emergence of a 'politicised fight culture' and the escalation of street violence (see Peter Beinart, 'The Rise of the Violent Left', *Atlantic*, September 2017). This is the worry shared by Evans and Reid when they argue that 'liberalism hides its own form of fascism' (Deleuze and Fascism, p. 5). Yet the appeal of Antifa has emerged from the realisation that neo-fascism is largely immune to appeals to reason, combined with the knowledge that hate speech against vulnerable minorities leads to real violence against them. In the terms the US Supreme Court has applied, Antifa understands neo-fascist hate speech as an incitement to violence and therefore as not protected by the First Amendment. So criticising Antifa is a little like blaming the victim for the violence involved in defending herself. And yet, there is a real worry here that Deleuze and Guattari are keen to diagnose, and that is the temptation to move from wresting power from the oppressor to consolidating that power in order to oppress others. This is what Foucault called becoming 'enamoured of power' ('Preface' to AO), and it is what Deleuze, Guattari, and the French left saw in the wake of the 1968 student/worker uprising. The suggestion that we all take a hard look at the fascism within the self is not a veiled call to pull back on real resistance to neo-fascism, it is a call to hold ourselves accountable for the ways in which we are and can become enamoured of power, self-destructively hateful, and reactive rather than active. In other words, for how our own lines of flight can become suicidal.
44. 'It is apparent acts of recognition exist and occupy a large part of our daily life: this is a table, this is an apple, this is a piece of wax, Good morning Theaetetus. But who can believe that the destiny of thought is at stake in these acts, and that when we recognise, we are thinking?' (DR 135).
45. James Williams, *Gilles Deleuze's* Difference and Repetition: *A Critical Introduction and Guide*, Edinburgh: Edinburgh University Press, 2003, p. 117.
46. All three of the reasons Deleuze gives for criticising recognition as a

deficient model for thought rely on a belief about the practical implications of uncritically accepting the dogmatic Image. The dogmatic Image of thought legitimates the feeling that what thinking is must be obvious to all because everyone possesses an identical and natural capacity to think. What should be obvious to any thinker [according to the dogmatic Image] is that thought is the natural expression of the harmony of all the faculties and has an 'affinity with the true' (DR 131). The dogmatic Image assumes that thinking is not naturally deceptive but true, reasonable, trustworthy and good. Recognisability is then used as a gauge by which true, reasonable, trustworthy and good thinking can be measured: the more recognisable it is, the truer and better the thinking. The motive for taking recognition as the model for all thought is to gain a strong starting point for establishing unassailable knowledge. Truer and better thinking produces well-founded and unquestionable knowledge. The dogmatic Image of thought is thus teleological in so far as its purpose is to achieve the pre-established practical goal of knowledge itself. While it may sound strange to say that knowledge is a practical goal, Deleuze's suggestion is rooted in the fundamentally Nietzschean contention that knowledge is never pure, abstract or unconnected to the development of particular hierarchies and value norms. Deleuze's contribution is to suggest that thought is capable of more than substantiating knowledge claims.

47. Deleuze's emphasis on the importance of the theory of faculties is in contrast with much of Kant scholarship. The notion of 'faculty' is ubiquitous in Kant's work but few readers have considered systematising its various uses, despite Kant's own emphasis on the importance and consistency of his use of faculties in the First Introduction to the *Critique of Judgement*.
48. For a helpful discussion of Deleuze's relationship to the post-Kantian project of metacritique, see Christian Kerslake, 'Deleuze, Kant, and the Question of Metacritique'. *Southern Journal of Philosophy* 42:4 (2004), pp. 481–508.
49. Inna Semetsky, 'Educating for 3C: Critical, Clinical, and Creative', conference presentation at the Philosophy of Education Society of Australasia, 2007, p. 3, at http://www.academia.edu/4273086/Educating_for_3C_Critical_Clinical_Creative (last accessed 1 February 2018).
50. Erinn Gilson, 'Responsive Becoming: Ethics Between Deleuze and Feminism', in *Deleuze and Ethics*, ed. Nathan Jun and Daniel Smith, Edinburgh: Edinburgh University Press, 2011, p. 74.
51. Rosi Braidotti, *Transpositions: On Nomadic Ethics*, Malden: Polity Press, 2006, p. 5.
52. Daniel Smith, 'The Place of Ethics in Deleuze's Philosophy: Three Questions of Immanence', in *Deleuze and Guattari: New Mappings*

in Politics, Philosophy, and Culture, ed. E. Kaufman and K. J. Heller, Minneapolis and London: University of Minnesota Press, 1998, p. 252.
53. Daniel W. Smith, 'Deleuze and the Question of Desire: Towards an Immanent Theory of Ethics', in *Deleuze and Ethics*, p. 124.
54. Smith, 'The Place of Ethics in Deleuze's Philosophy', p. 253.
55. Joe Barker, 'Love, Language, and the Dramatization of Ethical Worlds in Deleuze' *Deleuze Studies* 10:1 (2016), p. 100.
56. Smith, 'The Place of Ethics in Deleuze's Philosophy', p. 253.
57. Terence Lovat, Kerry Dally, Neville Clement and Ron Toomey, *Values, Pedagogy and Student Achievement: Contemporary Research Evidence*, New York: Springer, 2011, p. 36. As Rosi Braidotti puts it: a 'non-unitary subjectivity here means a nomadic, dispersed, fragmented vision, which is nonetheless functional, coherent and accountable, mostly because it is embedded and embodied' (*Transpositions*, p. 4).
58. Cf. Fritz Stern's appeal to a 'spirit of ebullient affirmation' in a talk he gave at the Leo Baeck Institute in 2005; at http://www.nytimes.com/cfr/international/20050501facomment_v84n3_stern.html?pagewanted=print&mcubz=3 (last accessed 28 September 2017).

PART I
Deleuze's Critical Philosophy – Kantian Critique and the Differential Theory of Faculties

1
The Deleuzian Subject

The Habit of Forming Habits

Perhaps, as Kristeva has suggested, the secret of ethical life is hidden in the stories we tell about ourselves. Whether these stories are told out loud and in groups or silently to ourselves is not what matters. What matters are the repetition of narrative tropes, the subtle expectations and exigencies they frame, the patterns woven through relationships, the creative investment in the process of narrating, and the simultaneous production of activity and expression of overlapping horizons of meaning. Of course, these stories are not entirely *sui generis*. They have an archetype. This archetype can be found in the story told about the formation of subjectivity. There is a wide appreciation in philosophy today that the story of the emergence of the subject is far richer and more complicated than the modern Western tradition has acknowledged. However, few if any contemporary philosophers have gone as far as Deleuze in freeing the story of the subject from its traditional rootedness in representational knowledge and identity.[1] For Deleuze, representational knowledge and identity are two of the implicit biases or 'subjective presuppositions' that have prejudiced the history of philosophy (DR 129). This prejudice has limited the possibilities of living that traditional philosophies can allow.

Like many French thinkers of the 1960s, Deleuze looked for real social and political change in resistance to the imperialistic and paternalistic styles of relating endemic to European culture. But the change Deleuze sought was more difficult to achieve than that of replacing a head of state (which is, of course, difficult enough in itself). So he conceived an entirely new ontology that would provide a novel set of stories capable of resisting the dogmatic biases of the past. As Deleuze saw things, beyond the ordered, formed being of the everyday there lies a sensible flux of 'energetic materiality' in continuous variation and development.[2] In other words, things are processes. In like manner, his theory of the subject emphasises its becoming in a never-ending process that refuses the exclusivity necessitated by identity and the common-sense presuppositions smuggled in by representational knowledge. While contemporary stories developing Deleuze's new ontology and his theory of the subject abound,[3] there is a distinct lack of stories focusing on the kind of life this subject should live.[4] This latter story – the story of a Deleuzian ethical life – is there, in the margins of his ontology, ready to be told and questioned, revised and supplemented. The key to its telling begins with the subject.

For Deleuze, the subject is not above or beyond the flux of the sensible. It does not stand as the calm and static eye at the centre of the hurricane. Rather, the subject is part of the flux. In contrast to hierarchical 'arborescent' models, Deleuze's subject is 'rhizomatic'; that is, it operates on the model of a continuously growing 'horizontal, subterranean stem', which sends out lateral shoots and adventitious roots at intervals along its length.[5] In *A Thousand Plateaus*, Deleuze and Guattari write that 'any point of a rhizome can be connected to any other, and must be' (TP 7). The subject exists, like everything else, as constituted in relationships and through relationships with the continually differentiating forces of becoming. As a result, the subject – or at this point more accurately a pre-subject – is fundamentally connected to all being through its becoming. Crucial to keep in mind is that this rhizomatic, relational pre-subject is itself in constant flux. For Deleuze, human existence is *mit-sein*, but even more so a multiplicity. Nomadic subjectivity is a consequence of Deleuze's reorientation of ontology in terms of the radical, inhuman forces of becoming, the pulse of immanence.

The subject begins its formation as an embryo, with all its latent powers of transformation. As Tamsin Lorraine writes in her inspiring study of Deleuze and Guattari's immanent ethics, subjects are 'evolving creatures struggling to unfold their capacities to live in always novel circumstances in response to life conceived as becoming'.[6] Subjects are changing, but these changes express a deep drive to use and develop their capacities. However, since the rhizome grows through connecting, the Deleuzo-Guattarian conception of the subject implies an ethics that appeals to the exigency of forming relationships as 'the immanent criterion of human flourishing'.[7] In Deleuze's story, the subject is a dynamic process, always in relation, always connected and connecting to others. Rather than understanding individuals as primarily autonomous things with essential attributes or fixed identities, in *A Thousand Plateaus* Deleuze and Guattari portray individuals through the Spinozist lens of what they can do and the relationships into which they can enter. Thus the ethical question is no longer how, why, or whether to connect to the world and those around us; as Lorraine notes, the issue is rather what 'kind of connections we want to foster and sustain'.[8] What connections will enrich the subject by opening it up to further growth and new connections? What connections will inspire action, creativity and self-transcendence? These are the pressing ethical questions Deleuze and Guattari's subject asks.

But how does such a dynamic, relational subject – one that nevertheless also exhibits enough stability to say 'I' – emerge from the flux of becoming? Deleuze's story about the subject does not begin with his collaborative work with Guattari. It even precedes his work in the late 1960s and early 1970s on Spinoza. The story begins with his first book, *Empiricism and Subjectivity* (1953), in which he proposes a near-Kantian reading of Hume's theory of subject formation. For Deleuze's Hume, the central question is how a collection becomes a system, or how the mind becomes a subject. From the empirical point of view, things are as they appear: 'a collection without an album, a play without a stage, a flux of perceptions' (ES 22–3). The embryonic flux, that collection of interconnected, rhizomatic fragments that Hume conceives in terms of a chaos of perceptions, emerges as a subject through the exercising of a certain capacity: the capacity to form habits. This starting point is crucial for any possible answer to the ethical question of which connections subjects should nurture. If for Deleuze there is 'no more striking answer to the problem of the Self' than the Humean one that 'we are habits, nothing but habits – the habit of saying "I"' (ES x), this suggests that the presupposition of identity is fundamental to subjective life in its everyday experience, even if this experience is secondary to the actual becoming that subjects are always in the process of undergoing. In a reference to Bergson, Deleuze specifies that these habits 'are not natural, but what is natural is the habit to take up habits' (ES 44). The subject's defining capacity is not the having of certain habits, but the habit of forming habits. The subject should therefore nurture those connections that will reinforce habits that foster qualities such as thinking, creativity and questioning – especially self-questioning. This will be key when it comes to articulating the ethical standpoint of resistance to dogmatic presuppositions. Even at this early moment in his oeuvre the necessity for a critique of the self is discernible in Deleuze's ethics.

Yet, this fundamental drive to habit-formation is passive. For Hume, the subject is passive and becomes activated through forming habits. Deleuze writes that when Hume speaks of an 'act of the mind', he does not mean that the mind is active but that 'it is activated and that it has become subject. The coherent paradox of Hume's philosophy is that it offers a subjectivity that transcends itself, without being any less passive' (ES 26). What Deleuze finds so striking about this Humean story is that the active/passive dichotomy is conceived as a false alternative. They are both accurate. The subject is an effect of habits or 'principles' sinking into the mind. As these habits congeal the subject becomes 'more and more active and less and less passive' (ES 112). Speaking in Bergsonian terms, Deleuze writes that 'the subject is an imprint, or an impression left by principles, that it progressively turns into a machine capable of using this impression' (ES 113). Lest it be thought that Deleuze's book on Hume were insignificant in the trajectory of his thinking, this early use of the term 'machine', which will become central to the later *Capitalism and Schizophrenia* project with Guattari, is telling. The machinic language is advantageous here in so far as it connotes a created thing governed by inner principles rather than its own intentionality. However, once it becomes active, the machine is 'capable of using' its own machinery – though this does not make it any less a machine (ES 113). In other words, the subject is passive but becomes capable of actively using its own passive processes. This is crucial because it allows the subject to take on a role in directing its own habit formation.[9]

This Humean theory of subjectivity is taken up as Deleuze's own (albeit with a far more distinctly Kantian overtone) in the development of the finite, constituting ego in the 1956 lectures that have recently been translated as *What is Grounding?* In these lectures, delivered at the lycée Louis le Grand prior to Deleuze's Assistant Professorship at the Sorbonne, subjectivity is constituted through unconscious processes or 'infinite tasks' that Deleuze describes as the 'real ends of reason' (WG 13–15). These ends are not to be realised, but must be 'undergone' (WG 18). They are discoverable when one ceases to 'relate one's activity to himself as an agent', and instead seeks 'the common subject in their acts (characters)' (WG 17). In other words, the 'real ends' of reason are discoverable when one ceases searching for the ground of ethics at the level of values and looks instead for the ground in the subjective principles or 'characters' that establish the value of values. The 'characters' described by Deleuze here bear a striking resemblance to the 'conceptual personae' he and Guattari discuss in Chapter 3 of *What is Philosophy?* (1991).

There, 'conceptual personae' are characterised as unique unities of apperception distinguishing different philosophies and their distinctive styles of thinking and living (the idiot, the schoolman, Socrates, Dionysus, and so on). They are neither entirely unconscious nor entirely conscious. They are neither entirely passive nor entirely active. They are 'halfway between concept and conceptual plane' (WP 61), occupying the space Kant reserved for transcendental conditions. If the rhizomatic subject can become capable of using its own passive, unconscious processes, it is through the selection and incorporation of these characters. An ethics here would replace the system of judgements with a system of affects.[10] The move to a more thoroughgoing Kantian language in Deleuze's early work is indicative of his direction even in the later collaborative work. When Deleuze and Guattari begin the third chapter of *What is Philosophy?* with a return to the theme of resistance to subjective presuppositions from *Difference and Repetition*, the move to unconscious processes echoes the same move Deleuze described as a departure from Hume's empiricism in favour of Kant's transcendental in *What is Grounding?*:

> Hume has posed the problem in general terms, but he has not responded to it. The principle seems psychological to him. In this sense, without Hume there would not have been Kant to retain the legitimacy of the ground. Kant will push the problem to the end and will go beyond this psychological interpretation. For Kant, the ground must be a subjective principle, but it cannot be psychological. It will be a transcendental subjectivity. (WG 13/27)

By going beyond the simple psychological in favour of a transcendental consciousness Kant is also able to avoid the Humean recourse to pre-established harmony in explaining how it is that nature abides the subjective going beyond of knowledge. By submitting the given to cognition, mental processes in Kant are no longer psychological because they no longer concern knowledge alone. Whence Kant's paradox: 'the ground is subjective, but it can no longer revolve around you and me ... it will account for [the fact] that the given submits itself to going beyond what I carry out' (WG 29). The submission of the given through unconscious, passive subjective processes is what Kant offers in the three syntheses of the A edition of the *Critique of Pure Reason*: the synthesis of apprehension in intuition, of reproduction in imagination, and of recognition in the concept. For critique, an exploration of the unconscious will be necessary. However, the true Kantian task is 'to replace the idea of method with an idea of formation', replacing the notion of critique as a method with the practice of critique as self-analysis that grounds cultivating transformation (WG 113).

What this Deleuzian story amounts to is that there is no single, unitary subject. There is something better: the infinite production of multiple, constantly evolving subjectivities. Deleuze's critique of the subject is not a complete rejection of the subject. While he does reject the notion of a subject assumed to be spontaneous, autonomous and unitary, he replaces this with a notion of the subject as passive, dissolved and fractured. Accordingly, 'the intentionality of being is surpassed by the fold of Being, Being as fold' (F 110). The notion of being as fold points toward a subjectivity understood as a process irreducible to universal notions such as totality, unity, or any prefixed self-identity. As a mode of intensity, subjectivity is capable of expressing itself in its present actuality neither by means of a progressive climbing toward the ultimate truth or a higher moral ideal, nor by 'looking for origins, even lost or deleted ones, but setting out to catch things where they were at work, in the middle: breaking things open, breaking words open' (N 86). This is important for Deleuze's story – it allows a pause in the narration; subjectivity is not one thing, it is never complete and does not hearken back to an original. Insofar as the subject is constituted around any pole, it is an arbitrary one that calls for analysis and re-analysis, for a tailoring to the vagaries of the real. This call motivates the necessity of self-narration and the illegitimacy of any outside narrative dependent on the category of the natural.

The search for an ethical standpoint buried within Deleuze's complex ontological story about the emergence of the subject from this flux of energetic materiality is grounded in ancient precedent, in at least two ways. It is a possibility that reaches at least as far back as the Heraclitean story of the close connection between a wise path in life and rational comprehension of *logos* as the maintenance of justice through opposition. However, the novelty Deleuze's story brings to this ancient archetype lies in its pauses. That is, the novelty is in part due to Deleuze's refusal to over-narrate the ethical life. While his work lays the theoretical groundwork for articulating what an ethical life based on critique could be, in this articulation his reticence to offer ethical directives allows readers the space to develop their own narratives. It is considered a risky move to allow the reader to fill in the details. When Mark Twain 'let us draw the curtain of charity over the rest of the scene' at the close of chapter 4 of *The*

Adventures of Tom Sawyer (1876), it was a vote cast in favour of the reader's imagination. In ethical theory this approach has been undervalued at best and rejected as a sure path to moral chaos at worst. Deleuze's ethics may not be ostentatious, but it does develop a set of insights that help orient ethical thinking. It emphasises the importance of returning to the ground, to one's starting points, to ask whether those starting points are or have become dogmatic biases. In Rosi Braidotti's terms, for this rhizomatic and 'nomadic' subject, resisting assimilation means inventing and creating new possibilities of life by going beyond the play of forces constitutive of subjectivity.[11] The ethical standpoint is thus constituted in the space of resistance, the space of the permanent revolution of the subject's own ways of thinking and living.

Fractural Anthropology

This story raises an important question: Does Deleuze's ethics depend on a particular anthropology or theory of human nature? The problem with ethical theories founded on particular anthropologies or theories of human nature is that they more or less subtly limit possibilities of life. On the more obvious side of the spectrum are those theories, such as Kant's, that seem to be founded on unproblematic starting points (such as the pure form of law-giving) but in reality rest on a theory of human nature that hierarchises people and ways of life according to a foundational anthropology based on the theorist's own biased assumptions. For Kant, this is visible in his perception of people's level of rationality – whereby women and people of colour are afforded a similar moral status to that of non-human animals and children. On the more subtle side of the spectrum, Charles Taylor's work on authenticity and Onora O'Neill's theory of inescapable vulnerability are also illustrative of this tendency.[12] Though Taylor takes great care to ground his phenomenological anthropology in an analysis of the cultivation of autonomy, and O'Neill begins with a persuasive argument centred on establishing the 'universal' experience of vulnerability, both ultimately establish a conservative, elitist ethics based on a particular anthropology.[13] A little more detail on this point will serve to illuminate Deleuze's ethics by way of distinction.

While Taylor defends the ideal of authenticity, he does so by connecting it to what he and others see as a corrosive individualism propped up by the sort of relativism that leads to self-satisfaction, small-mindedness and complacency.[14] His defence of authenticity refers the concept to a Rousseauian inner moral 'voice' or *sentiment de l'existence*' at the core of being. This inner voice expresses the subject's nature, or, in Herder's terms, its own 'measure' or originality.[15] Getting in touch with one's own unique, original voice is what the ethics of authenticity strives for. Yet, from a Deleuzian perspective, the point of view of authenticity treats the subject itself uncritically. Authenticity seeks to uncover the genuine, unique voice or conscience within each person, but offers no resources for distinguishing what is authentic from what is subjective bias, or for multiplying voices so as to expand the self into manifold, unfamiliar, or even challenging perspectives. Taylor's commitment to excavating a single, true authentic voice within individual subjects has the effect of limiting what counts as authentic. In O'Neill's case, she, like Kant, ultimately wants to corral the forces of becoming into a theory of human nature – albeit a minimal one that begins with the acknowledgement of shared vulnerability – whereby she can reassert the traditional universalisability test of moral principles. From Deleuze's perspective, this return to the Kantian test of universalisability, which demands that principles be based on reasons that everyone could accept, takes common sense and all of the subjective biases wrapped up within it as the ground of moral reasonableness. While both of these theories make strides toward a genuinely critical ethics, they are limited in their relevance to thinking creatively about the most pressing contemporary ethical issues, in which the non-human world – the world of those traditionally excluded from 'universal' views – has taken shape as an horizon of deep significance. One of the most important contributions to ethics that a Deleuzian story can offer is a theory that is not founded on a restrictive anthropology, whether of an obvious or a subtle variety.

It is then of crucial importance to demonstrate that a Deleuzian ethics avoids this particular problem of assuming an anthropology that smuggles in subjective presuppositions. Though the story of Deleuze's relationship to his own subjective presuppositions will become more complicated as it unfolds, in order to begin to show how unique his theory of subjectivity and the ethics that can be derived from it are, it is necessary to take a closer look at his use of the theory of faculties he finds in Kant. In the language Deleuze uses in his synthesis of Kant's three critiques, *Kant's Critical Philosophy* (1963), in his *Proust and Signs* (1964), as well as in his ground-breaking book *Difference and Repetition* (1968), the capacities for habit formation, as well as for memory, image, and thought formation, are referred to as 'faculties'. Faculties express powers of both activity and passivity. Deleuze connects his earlier Humean story of the subject emergent from the flux of becoming through habit-formation to a Kantian model of faculties as passive and active capacities. While the Humean theory of subjectivity is a touchstone for Deleuze, his debt to Kant's theory of faculties is arguably more fundamental to the articulation of his own story in so far as the language of faculties provides a structure connecting the ontology with the theory of subjectivity that carries through all the way from *Difference and Repetition* to the *Capitalism and Schizophrenia* project with Guattari. Though this connecting theme has been largely underappreciated in the scholarship, Joe Hughes has argued brilliantly for a subterranean thread holding Deleuze's oeuvre together centred on the process of synthesis emerging from the theory of faculties.[16] While the typical reading of Deleuze's relationship to Kant turns on the idea that he required an empiricist reversal of the critical philosophy – whereby the Kantian question of how the given can be given to a subject would become the Humean question of how the subject can be constituted within the given – in light of the depth of the Kantian influence within Deleuze's reading of Hume, as well as the account of the passivity of the 'I' in the passive synthesis of Time, it is clear that any adequate treatment of the power of synthesis must go by way of the larger account of the faculties.

Though Deleuze does not define the notion of faculty in the pages of *Difference and Repetition*, he follows the Kantian model of conceiving faculties as relations of power operating at the transcendental level (DR 143–4).[17] Such an understanding of faculties as relations of power not only complements Deleuze's 'energetic' ontology (DR 240, 243), early in *Difference and Repetition* he synonymises 'faculty' with 'function' (DR 15) – a word that refers to the activity particular to some category of things, especially of 'the moral and intellectual powers'.[18] Moreover, it is important to note that in following Kant onto the transcendental level, Deleuze believes he is following him onto a pre-subjective level. Faculties do not belong to subjects, rather, as Levi Bryant puts it, 'subjects are precipitated from faculties . . . [and] these faculties are none other than the tendencies characterizing being. They are the differentials or joints of being itself, and not faculties of a subject's mind.'[19] Recall that in *Difference and Repetition*, thought conceived under the dogmatic Image is supposed to be naturally true, reasonable, trustworthy and good because it is the expression of the harmony of all the faculties under the common sense as *concordia facultatum*. In the history of philosophy proceeding from Aristotle, the *concordia facultatum* is derived from the presupposition that there is a natural unity of the subject that grounds the harmony of the faculties. After all, what is more obvious – more commonsensical – than that the whiteness the faculty of sight sees becomes connected to the sweetness the faculty of taste tastes through their both belonging to the same subject? This is analogous to Kant's unity of apperception (CPR B127). The unitary subject establishes the unity of experience. The strategy behind Deleuze's emphasis on a theory of faculties now becomes clearer: to create real thought freed from the constraints of the dogmatic Image, the real interplay of faculties constitutive of common sense beneath the supposed unity of the subject must be revealed. In other words, in order to free thought from its subjective presuppositions, we must start by conceiving thinking on a pre-subjective level. The power of synthesis is the power of identity formation, so a theory of synthesis that subverts the necessity of an assumed and common-sense harmony is fundamental to Deleuze's larger project.

In a more recent article, Bryant goes so far as to suggest that instead of thinking of the faculties as belonging to a transcendental subject, we should instead consider them as belonging to a 'transcendental field'.[20] This is in keeping with the move Deleuze makes in his later works when he argues for an 'impersonal and pre-individual' transcendental field in which the subject is conceived as an identity pole that produces its identities through active syntheses which are themselves the product of passive syntheses. As Daniel Smith and John Protevi put it: the syntheses of habit happen through contractions which unify sets of experience extracting what will be retained and allowing the rest to be 'forgotten'. Together, the various bodily passive syntheses form a differential, transcendental field in which 'subjects' are 'the patterns of these multiple, serial syntheses which fold in on themselves producing a site of self-awareness'.[21] Because Deleuze regards the faculties as being what underlies the supposed unity of the subject, they must be understood not as mental phenomena but as the expressions of the dynamic forces underlying those phenomena. Even though he does not give his readers a formal definition, it is clear that Deleuze understands the faculties in terms of the forces or powers they instantiate. The Humean influence remains, but the theory of faculties becomes central to the unfolding of the pre-subject. As Kristensen puts it: 'the constitution of the subject should not be thought of as a mental state. It is not the subject that is the fact of knowledge. Hence it is not the active already constituted subject of psychology that constitutes the world within which the subject lives.'[22]

However, in emphasising Deleuze's reliance on Kant, who quite explicitly and infamously proposed a theory of human nature to flesh out the practical critique, Deleuze's reading of Kant must be shown to be anything but traditional.[23] This poses a delicate problem in relation to the issue of anthropology, since Deleuze's story of the faculties appears at first blush to model a psychology of the mind. This is an issue that has troubled Kant scholarship for decades.[24] Returning to Deleuze's reading of Hume, he argues that 'Hume's project entails the *substitution of a psychology of the mind by a psychology of the mind's affections*' (ES 21). The psychology of the mind's affections, which Deleuze takes up as the theory of faculties, 'gave the *association* of ideas its real meaning, making it a practice of cultural and *conventional* formations . . . rather than a theory of the human mind' (ES ix). Faculties do not express a human nature, they express the power of time and repetition within particular cultural heritages found in the forces of language, history, social and political mechanics, and 'images of thought'. While the faculties do concern the mind in so far as human subjects are the matter under analysis, the faculties are not limited to the mind and do not originate in the mind, as would a human nature. Deleuze and Guattari's later abandonment of the language of faculties in favour of the language of machines illustrates the importance they placed on avoiding a psychologistic anthropomorphism of faculties. Yet, this later change in language does not mean that the earlier theory of faculties failed, only that the language of machines went further in removing the need for any psychologism.

The anti-psychologism inherent in Deleuze's use of the language of faculties is clear enough given that one of the primary motives behind his conceiving the faculties in terms of relations of force rather than mental phenomena was his refusal to follow Kant into the 'psychologism' for which his critique has been condemned by generations of scholars.[25] 'Psychologism', as Deleuze describes it, is the problem of deriving transcendental principles from simple empirical examples (DR 135). If – so the criticism goes – what the transcendental is supposed to mark out are the conditions of experience, Kant's critique falls short in so far as he derives those conditions from experience itself. After all, the conditions of experience may in no way resemble actual experience. Deleuze explains it like this:

> of all philosophers, Kant is the one who discovers the prodigious domain of the transcendental . . . However, what does he do? In the first edition of the *Critique of Pure Reason* he describes in detail three syntheses which measure the respective contributions of the thinking faculties, all culminating in the third, that of recognition, which is expressed in the form of the unspecified object as correlate of the 'I think' to which all the faculties are related. It is clear that, in this manner, Kant traces the so-called transcendental structures from the empirical acts of a psychological consciousness . . . In order to hide this all too obvious procedure, Kant suppressed this text in the second edition. Although it is better hidden, the tracing method, with all its 'psychologism', nevertheless subsists. (DR 135)

Even though Kant discovers the level of the transcendental, he is unable to remain at that level when he refers the relationship between the transcendental faculties to the immediacy of recognition on the empirical and psychological level of self-consciousness. The active synthetic identity of the 'I think', which Kant relies on to establish a relationship between the faculties, is simply what Deleuze diagnosed as the 'common sense as *concordia facultatum*' (DR 133). When Kant falls back on what he presumes is the empirical obviousness of the unity of our self-consciousness, Deleuze claims, he renounces his transcendental critique just short of putting into question the most basic of his presuppositions: common sense itself. As such, Kant's critique can only go so far as common sense will allow.[26] In practical terms, the problem of 'psychologism' is that since the empirical is given under the form of common sense, using the empirical as the model for the conditions of experience only transposes common sense into those conditions – with all of the conventions and conservativeness that it inherits from requiring the recognisability of anything that is to count as thought. A transposition of this sort not only serves as an in-principle standard by which to impose conformity on people (by legitimising only one way of experiencing the world: the way deemed true, reasonable, trustworthy and good according to the standard of recognition), it also impedes any appreciation of the real conditions of experience, and likewise the real conditions of common sense and of thought without Image. Thus the problem of 'psychologism' echoes the problem of subjective presuppositions: both operate through a return to what was already known implicitly at the start and so foreclose any venturing into the unknown.

This is why Deleuze is invested in separating Kant's understanding of the faculties from any 'subjective' reading that would treat them as psychological features of the mind. Despite the seeming anthropomorphism implied in Kant's attribution of 'ends' and 'interests' to the faculties, Deleuze argues that his 'transcendental' faculties are expressions of the dynamic forces or relations of power (*Vermögen*) underlying the psychological phenomena subjects subjectively experience. This is consistent with Deleuze's understanding of Kant's faculties as the subject's capacities for experience, and their difficult inter-relation as forming the basis of experience, error, illusion, faith and knowledge. It is this sense of faculties as relations of power that Deleuze then adopts and revises in *Difference and Repetition*.

In that work Deleuze claims that the faculties are organised serially, and in keeping with the standpoint of empiricism he locates sensibility at the origin of the series.[27] However, in privileging sensibility he does not mean to locate the origin of thought in our relation to everyday empirical experiences, as these are always necessarily given under the form of common sense. Whereas everyday empirical experiences are already representations, 'sensations' in Deleuze's sense are 'sub-representative' and immediate affects (DR 57). Like Kant's manifold of intuition (the forms of sensibility of space and time [CPR A77/B102]), Deleuze's 'sensations' are intuitive yet undergo their own 'passive syntheses' before relating with the active syntheses that make up representational experience and thought (DR 71–5). Unlike Kant's manifold of intuition, the passive syntheses constitutive of Deleuze's 'sensations' are not the forms of space and time, but the 'contractions' of habit that 'are not carried out *by* the mind, but happen *in* the mind' (DR 71). So, rather than locate the origin of thought in empirical experience *or* in the forms of that experience, Deleuze identifies the origin of both thought and sensations in 'Difference' or 'intensity' (DR 236–7).

Of course, Deleuze's notions of 'Difference' and 'intensity' specify not simple empirical differences but that which makes empirical differences possible. While empirical differences are external to sensations (as well as to faculties and representations), in so far as they serve to separate sensations from one another, Difference is internal and establishes an a priori relation between them. For example, this book on the desk is different from that book on the shelf. They are different in innumerable ways: they have different sizes, different colours, they were written by different people, and so on. All of these differences are simple empirical differences in so far as the differences marked out are external to the books themselves. Difference itself, on the other hand, is the basic ontological level of pure diversity that makes it possible for empirical differences between books to come into being at all. It would be a mistake to associate Difference with the concept of the 'between', however, as such a move would prioritise identity in the definition of Difference – something Deleuze is keen to avoid. Instead, Difference must be understood as that which makes the diversity of experience be as it is, which produces diversity and allows it to manifest itself. That is why Deleuze refers to Difference as internal. It is internal to each book, each tree, each person, and each idea, rather than just distinguishing between books, trees, people and ideas. Difference is also the origin and limit of sensibility and it is Difference's immediate relationship to sensation that explains sensibility's priority in Deleuze's differential theory of faculties. Difference is the origin in so far as it is the intensive level out of which sensations and even the faculty of sensibility are born. But Difference is also the limit of sensibility in so far as Difference is 'imperceptible' from the point of view of common sense (DR 140). This is why another of Deleuze's ways of characterising it is as 'what can *only* be sensed', or even more mysteriously, as an 'encounter' (DR 243; 139).

Deleuze's description of the difference between 'the Kantian and the Cartesian Cogito' illustrates well the difference between faculties as relations of power and as simple mental phenomena (DR 85). Deleuze begins drawing this difference by suggesting that Descartes' Cogito be conceived as operating on two poles: the 'I think' (or, 'the determination') and the 'I am' (or 'the undetermined'). For Descartes the 'I think' is so immediate and spontaneous that it must be the attribute of a substantial being. That is, the determination ('I think') directly implies the substantiality of our undetermined existence ('I am') because, obviously, in order to think one must exist. Descartes' Cogito is simply the expression of the mental phenomenon of the obviousness of thought's good nature and immediate relation to existence (i.e. of the dogmatic Image of thought). What Kant realises, Deleuze explains, is that it would be impossible for the determination to bear directly on the undetermined without some kind of mediation that would allow the undetermined to be determinable. Deleuze is keen on the idea of 'the determinable' because, for him, it is the moment of the discovery of the transcendental. Indeed, Deleuze writes, the idea of the determinable 'amounts to the discovery of Difference' (DR 86). Kant discovers 'a transcendental Difference between the Determination as such and what it determines; no longer in the form of an external difference which separates, but in the form of an internal Difference which establishes an a priori relation between thought and being' (DR 86). The moment of Kant's realisation that thought cannot determine being without the establishment of an a priori relationship between them is the moment of the inception of the transcendental as the level of a priori relations. One could add that the discovery of the necessity of a priori determinability between thought and existence is also the discovery of the idea of faculties as relations of power. The determinable mediates between the two poles of determination and the undetermined, but it is not itself a pole. Deleuze writes that the 'transcendental principle does not govern any domain but gives the domain to be governed to a given empirical principle; it accounts for the subjection of a domain to a principle' (DR 241). Moreover, determinability is the capacity or power through which the undetermined is able to be determined. The determinable therefore expresses a relation of power or capacity. Faculties are enumerations of determinability based on the different sources of different kinds of representations. Faculties understood in this way are thus a far cry from the Cartesian Cogito's experience of simple mental phenomena – however subject to reflection those phenomena may be.

Yet, while in *Kant's Critical Philosophy* Deleuze attributes to Kant two definitions of faculty – 'faculties of mind', which express types of relations between representations and their object or subject,[28] and 'faculties', which express the source of representations[29] – he adopts only the latter in *Difference and Repetition*. Understanding why this should be is a complicated story. It begins with Deleuze's identification of Kant's 'faculties of mind' as expressions of particular ends or interests of the faculty of Reason, not of the faculties of understanding or imagination (KCP 3). Indeed, according to Deleuze, what defines philosophy for Kant is the analysis of the relationship between Reason and its ends. Deleuze admires the immanent perspective exhibited in this definition, even though for him philosophy is not defined in terms of understanding and facilitating Reason's proper self-relationship but in terms of realising thought's power of breaking with *doxa* through the achievement of a thought without Image and the creation of genuinely new concepts (DR 134; cf. WP 79). To that end, not only is Deleuze interested in faculties other than Reason, he also conceives of the true 'end' of each faculty as the realisation of that faculty's highest internal power. That is why Deleuze's critical philosophy is not carried out at the level of conditions of experience but at the level of the genesis of thinking as it is achieved through each faculty's attainment of its own distinctive higher form. Deleuze conceives of this shift from conditioning to genesis as consistent with the original spirit of Kant's critical project, which he considers to have been worked out at its most profound level in the *Critique of Judgement*, where Kant provides a genetic account of the development of aesthetic common sense.

Deleuze's reading of the failure of the critical project in *Kant's Critical Philosophy* suggests that Kant's predetermination of Reason's interests smuggles in moral interests. Faculties express a deep passivity of the mind. Time, as the form of inner sense, is constitutive of a subject that does not have a self-identical moment at its foundation. The founding moment of Deleuze's subject is a fracture within the self. Time has an important function in the constitution of subjectivity, and subjectivity is essentially linked with practice: the problem can only be correctly raised at the level of practice. What would an ethical practice built on passivity and fracture look like? The first thing to note is that this theory is distinct from Cartesian and phenomenological theories of subjectivity; most importantly from theories that represent the I as static, atomistic, teleological, 'common sense', or even 'authentic'. Deleuze's mature philosophical work poses a striking criticism of modern notions of the subject, particularly on the point of its substantiality or any invocation of subterranean 'authenticity' tied to notions of human nature. Moreover, the unconscious enfolded in subjectivity entails the insufficiency of interpreting subjectivity in terms of the stable identity of the rational and intentional subject, or some ideal and authentic self. The unconscious, pre-conceptual plane is always productive and constructive, making subjectivity transient and movable. While it may be controversial to call Deleuze's work anti-phenomenological, in so far as it breaks with the model of representation inherent in phenomenology's reliance on intentionality, it is illustrative to return to distinguishing his approach from the phenomenological one suggested by Charles Taylor.

The problem with Taylor's ontology of the 'authentic self' is that his conception of the subject is based on a certain interpretation of what critical practice is. In short, Taylor's phenomenological conception of the subject depends on understanding Kantian critical practice as purely epistemological, so that it is necessarily the case that the only way to proceed from Kant is to phenomenology. For Taylor's argument to work, he must connect Kant's transcendental conditions with conditions of intentionality. But what he does not appreciate is that Kant's critique has an ontological dimension. Likewise, what he does not anticipate in his criticism of Foucault and Derrida is another 'neo-Nietzschean' thinker whose work on Kant can be read as a challenge to subjectivist conceptions of the Kantian theory of faculties and to epistemological readings of critique. Deleuze's early work, from *Empiricism and Subjectivity* through *Difference and Repetition*, offers precisely such a reading. Deleuze suggests that Kant's practice of critique be understood as *immanent*, and that his recurrent descriptions of the relationships between the faculties of thought be understood as proposing a theory of relations of forces that underlie the genesis of the subject. It is by bringing to light Kant's demand for an immanent critique, along with the hitherto underappreciated unity of his account of pre-subjective faculties, that Deleuze connects Kantian critique with an ontology that is inseparable from an ethos. Deleuze uses this immanent critical ethos as the implicit practical 'method' of *Difference and Repetition*, developing it further in the *Capitalism and Schizophrenia* books, and completing it in *What is Philosophy?*[30] In contrast to Taylor's ontology of the 'authentic self', Deleuze's critique, understood as an ethos of evaluation, does not presuppose a foundational anthropology that would limit possibilities of life. Rather, his critique is built on a fractural anthropology that requires the evaluation of all presuppositions and arouses life to expand to the very limits of its power.

Dangerous Habits

The danger of this Deleuzian story about the passive subject's activation through habits is that habits can sediment into blockages against the very thinking for which they are the condition. Habits become settled tendencies through their regular practice, despite the fracture at the core of the self. The problem is that this regular practice more often than not happens through unchosen and unconscious mechanisms. Yet, the dispositions they create are vital to the production of the subject's thoughts and actions, indeed, to any possibility of a story about freedom and agency. If the practices adopted are ones that do not question the representational model of thinking, that repeat cultural stereotypes uncritically, or internalise an atomistic view of individuals in society, then they create a conservative disposition allergic to the power of becoming. For the empirical subject, this danger is the very real one of stagnating in life.

The Deleuzian story thus has clear resonances with the Sartrean story about the nothingness at the heart of being and the preferability of choosing the life of the for-itself over that of the in-itself. But whereas the existentialist story takes the starting point in radical freedom as axiomatic, the Deleuzo-Guattarian story begins in the fullness of being that individuates as a result of passive forces sedimenting into habits. And while both of these stories are radical and powerful departures from the hierarchical stories favoured in the history of philosophy, the Deleuzo-Guattarian version departs from the language of authenticity, the recourse to personal responsibility, and the tendency of identity politics to exclusivity that have shadowed existentialism. Instead, it refocuses attention on the macro-systems of power that create the conditions of possibility for particular identities – that produce the habits constitutive of those identities.[31]

If habits are malleable, perhaps the constituted identities they form can be altered, subverted, or even created anew. In the Kantian language Deleuze takes up post-*Empiricism and Subjectivity*, habits are conceived as syntheses and produced through the operation of certain faculties or powers. These syntheses are both passive and active, with the passive syntheses – beginning with the synthesis of habit – preceding the active ones. In *Philosophy After Deleuze*, Joe Hughes points out that 'a passive synthesis is one which is pre-conceptual and does not have recourse to concepts . . . [therefore], there is no law regulating them'.[32] In other words, passive syntheses are not subject to rules. They are free. However, through the intervention of the ideas of good sense and common sense, the passive faculties become active, individuating particular identities based on the law of representation in the process. If this process is capable of forming subjects with dispositions toward conservatism in thinking, then it should also be capable of forming subjects who bear within themselves the power of becoming out of which they emerged.

Deleuze offers such a possibility in his discussion of the process of dramatisation, which is a term he utilises to discuss an aesthetic practice of critique in his early works, particularly in his 1967 essay 'The Method of Dramatization' and in *Difference and Repetition*. Didier Debaise has argued that since transformation is part of a generalised function of granting events the importance they call for, dramatisation operates as the intensification of the importance of events through an inversion of habitual thinking. This inversion is a difficult process that requires an askesis of thought.[33] Through the process of dramatisation, Ideas turn subjects 'into larvae' that 'bear Ideas in their flesh', radically reshaping that flesh (DR 272).

Dramatisation harnesses the power of Ideas to alter habits at the level of the passive syntheses. Of course, as Hughes notes

> if Deleuze's images here all evoke some kind of shimmering violence, it is because dramatisation brings the rules of the Idea to bear on the passive processes of larval subjects. In other words, in the same way that the Kantian schematism worked by co-opting the imagination's synthesis, the Deleuzian drama returns to the body and redirects its syntheses.[34]

Ideas re-form the individualised subject by co-opting the passive syntheses. In other words, subjects' habits can change by changing their ideas. This insight is even more developed in *Anti-Oedipus* where Deleuze and Guattari show that 'the territorial stage of social production functions by co-opting all three of the passive syntheses'.[35]

The insight that Ideas formed through the aesthetic practice of critique (dramatisation) can reshape the subject at the passive level of habit has enormous implications. It is important to note, however, that in order for the practice of critique not to merely repeat the form of good sense/common sense, it must not itself be based on any rule or concept of recognition given in advance. The principle of critique as 'eternal return' provides the outline for such a criteria: the selection of forces that is invented through an active (rather than reactive) will. In *Nietzsche and Philosophy* Deleuze associates this invention with an art of self-destruction that transcends the passivity of the self and its habits of thinking. Ethics arises in the moment of crisis when a principle adequate to the situation must be invented. The principle, a purely formal 'cultivating idea', goes like this: 'If, in all that you will you begin by asking yourself: is it certain that I will do it an infinite number of times? This should be your solid center of gravity' (NP 37). In an excellent passage that deserves to be quoted without interruption, Hughes describes the process like this:

> In this moment, thinking becomes properly active, and its activity is manifested in a fundamental creativity. While Deleuze does not emphasise this, we might notice that thought becomes free here in two senses. It is free, first of all, in the break it makes from passivity through the process of active self-destruction. It is no longer subject to the play of forces at the level of the body. It is free second of all in the sense that thought here invents its own law. It becomes autonomous. This is what Deleuze does emphasise. The thought of the eternal return 'makes willing a creation' (80), and transforms our will into an 'artistic will' which fully realises its activity through a process of 'selection, correction, redoubling, and affirmation' in which it formulates a 'practical rule' (81). When Deleuze

says that the thought of the eternal return opens up the 'possibility of transmutation as a new way of feeling, thinking, and above all being' (82), then, we need to understand this in two ways. The 'possibility of transmutation' is secured by our freedom from passivity; the new ways of feeling which are invented in this rupture are the productions of thought as a creative faculty which gives itself its own law.[36]

The story of a practice of active habit formation that is beyond rules is the ethical model buried within Deleuze's practice of critique. If subjects express the habit of making habits, the practice of critique creates new habits based on a non-Image of thought. This is an aesthetic-ethical practice – an ethos – of imagination, creativity and affirmation. It is a way of resisting the dogmatism or fascism of subjective presuppositions by developing habits of self-critique. The contractions of habit can be understood in two ways: as the synthesis of two opposing elements (tick-tock) but also as the synthesis of syntheses that form the habits of living within a contemplative soul (one's ethos). As Deleuze writes, 'It is simultaneously through contraction that we are habits, but through contemplation that we contract' (DR 74). Selection and contemplation – two processes that depend on an analysis of the faculties – go hand in hand in forming the habits of living that create and recreate the subject. Whereas in Kant critique is the nearly paradoxical idea of the self-evaluation of reason by reason, Deleuze transforms it into the nearly paradoxical practice of the self-evaluation of faculties. Unlike for psychologists – who, Deleuze argues, conceive of habits as formed through acting – Deleuze wonders whether 'the self itself is a contemplation . . . whether we can learn, form behaviour and form ourselves other than through contemplation' of the real powers and limits of the faculties (DR 73). In fact, there is no other truth for Deleuze than 'the creation of the New: creativity, emergence' (CII 147), or giving shape to one's existence through self-critique, rather than attempting to discover its eternal and invariant form.

Notes

1. Indeed, including his work with Guattari, the Oedipalised and anthropocentric model of subjectivity are also contested.
2. Daniel Smith, 'Deleuze's Theory of Sensation: Overcoming the Kantian Duality', in *Deleuze: A Critical Reader*, ed. Paul Patton, Oxford: Blackwell, 1996, p. 43.
3. Rosi Braidotti's *Nomad Subjects*, New York: Columbia University Press, 1994, is probably the best known of these.

4. Erinn Gilson's *The Ethics of Vulnerability*, New York: Routledge, 2014, is a beautifully written exception.
5. Cf. the *OED Online* definition for 'rhizome'.
6. Tamsin Lorraine, *Deleuze and Guattari's Immanent Ethics*, Albany: SUNY, 2011, p. vii.
7. Ibid.
8. Ibid. p. 12.
9. The idea being developed here of a form of habit that resists fascistic habits is in contrast to the understanding of habit that Braidotti expresses when she writes that 'the force of habit is indeed little more than inertia, that is to say a reactive type of affect. "Habits" are a socially enforced and thereby "legal" type of addiction. They are cumulated toxins which by sheer uncreative repetition engender forms of behaviour that can be socially accepted as "normal" or even "natural"' (*Transpositions*, p. 9). Though Braidotti is an ally when it comes to creating an ethical vision she puts more emphasis on the forces that push us out of habits rather than on the character traits one might develop to cultivate an openness to those encounters.
10. See Smith, 'The Place of Ethics in Deleuze's Philosophy'.
11. Braidotti, *Nomad Subjects*, p. 22.
12. Charles Taylor, *The Ethics of Authenticity*, Cambridge, MA: Harvard University Press, 1991; Onora O'Neill, *Towards Justice and Virtue: A Constructive Account of Practical Reasoning*, Cambridge: Cambridge University Press, 1996.
13. See especially Taylor's chapter on 'Atomism' in *Philosophy and the Human Sciences*, p. 192.
14. See especially chapter 2 of Taylor's *The Ethics of Authenticity*, 'The Inarticulate Debate'.
15. Taylor, *The Ethics of Authenticity*, p. 27.
16. See Joe Hughes, *Philosophy After Deleuze*, London: Bloomsbury, 2012, pp. 14–19.
17. Deleuze developed his reading of Kant at the same time as he was writing his book on Nietzsche. The latter also understood the Kantian theory of faculties as a theory of forces, Deleuze implies, when Nietzsche describes the 'faculty of forgetting' as an 'active force' (NP 115).
18. Cf. the *OED Online* definition for 'function'.
19. Levi Bryant, *Difference and Givenness*, Chicago: Northwestern University Press, 2008, p. 97.
20. Levi Bryant, 'Deleuze's Transcendental Empiricism: Notes Towards a Transcendental Materialism', in *Thinking Between Deleuze and Kant: A Strange Encounter*, ed. Edward Willatt and Matt Lee, New York: Continuum, 2009, p. 45.
21. Daniel Smith and John Protevi, 'Gilles Deleuze', in *The Stanford Encyclopedia of Philosophy* (Winter 2015 edition), ed. Edward

N. Zaita, at https://plato.stanford.edu/archives/win2015/entries/deleuze (last accessed 1 February 2018).
22. Kristensen, 'Thinking Normativity in Deleuze's Philosophy', p. 15.
23. Ethics is inherent in this story about the production of subjectivity. As Deleuze writes, subjectivation is 'ethical and aesthetic' (*Negotiations 1972–1990*, trans. Martin Joughin, New York: Columbia University Press, 1995, p. 114). The ethical and the aesthetic are notions that he opposes to 'morality'. Deleuzian philosophy always speaks of values that are to come. This theory of the subject is the ground of an ethical practice as cultivation of moral judgement through habits. The artist-philosopher does not conjure things out of thin air. As Keith Ansell-Pearson puts it: 'their compositions are only possible because they are able to connect, to tap into the virtual and immanent processes of machinic becoming . . . One can only seek to show the power, the affectivity, the . . . alienated character of thought, which means being true to thought and untrue to oneself. One . . . is drawn to the land of the always near-future' (Keith Ansell-Pearson, *Deleuze and Philosophy: The Difference Engineer*, New York: Routledge, 1997, p. 4).
24. See Ralf Meerbote, 'Deleuze on the Systematic Unity of the Critical Philosophy', *Kant-Studien* 77 (1986), pp. 347–54. Meerbote argues that Deleuze's account of the systematicity of the critical project provides a helpful framework and emphasises similarities between the critiques (such as common sense) that have not previously been identified but that bear close investigation. However, Meerbote, like many Kant scholars, misunderstands Deleuze's interpretation of the faculties, taking them to be empirico-psychological aspects of the mind.
25. For example, Hermann Cohen, Paul Natorp and Michel Foucault all saw 'psychologism' as the primary weakness of Kant's work.
26. 'However, in spite of everything, and at the risk of compromising the conceptual apparatus of the three Critiques, Kant did not want to renounce the implicit presuppositions. Thought had to continue to enjoy an upright nature, and philosophy could go no further than – nor in directions other than those taken by – common sense' (DR 136).
27. 'It is true that on the path which leads to that which is to be thought, all begins with sensibility' (DR 144).
28. These are the faculty of knowledge, the faculty of desire and the faculty of the feeling of pleasure and pain (KCP 3–4).
29. These are Imagination, understanding and Reason (KCP 8–9).
30. This analysis is in broad agreement with Miguel De Beistegui's association of schizoanalysis with Kantian critique in *Immanence: Deleuze and Philosophy*, Edinburgh: Edinburgh University Press, 2010, pp. 118–22.
31. See Lois McNay, *Foucault and Feminism: Power, Gender, and the Self*, Cambridge: Polity, 1992. Debates around subject-formation that lie at the heart of philosophical discussions of identity politics parallel

debates between Habermasians and Foucauldians about the possibility of a transcendental subject that would ground practices of critique. See Amy Allen, *The Politics of Our Selves*, New York: Columbia University Press, 2008.
32. Hughes, *Philosophy After Deleuze*, p. 33.
33. Didier Debaise, 'The Dramatic Power of Events', *Deleuze Studies* 10:10 (2016), p. 7.
34. Hughes, *Philosophy After Deleuze*, p. 52.
35. Ibid. p. 53.
36. Hughes, *Philosophy After Deleuze*, p. 73. Page references in the quotation refer to Deleuze, *Nietzsche and Philosophy*.

2

The Theory of Faculties

The broadly Kantian perspective woven into Deleuze's reading of the Humean story of the subject's emergence from the flux of becoming through the sedimentation of habits is at bottom a story about the unfolding drama of the relationship between passive and active faculties. In his early work, Deleuze employs the notion of the faculties in order to ask the question of what bodies can do. The analysis of the faculties, of the passive syntheses that become activated through the recursivity of Ideas, reveals simultaneously the constituting forces of common sense and the vital, revolutionary forces of thinking. This is fundamental to the project of philosophy itself, conceived by Deleuze as the contestation of *doxa* through the creation of concepts. In his book on *Foucault*, Deleuze asks, 'What is philosophy today ... if it is not the critical work that thought brings to bear on itself? In what does it consist, if not in the endeavour to know how and to what extent it is possible to think differently, instead of legitimating what is already known?' (F 8–9).

Of course, this story has multiple layers, none of which should be ignored. Everything from Deleuze's reclamation of a 'minor' history of philosophy, to the material conditions of his life, to the art, science and mathematics that formed his cultural and intellectual milieu are indispensable for appreciating the richness and complexity of his stories. Here, the layer under investigation is primarily the Kantian one. However, in bringing to light the radical practice of critique woven throughout Deleuze's work, it is also necessary to confront the possibility of its Kantian contamination. The reason for this is simple and widely appreciated. Taking Kant's philosophy as one's starting point introduces a number of problematic assumptions into one's own work. It is impossible, as Robert Bernasconi has eloquently argued, to analytically split off the preferred part of Kant's work without bringing the Eurocentric, racist and misogynist parts with it.[1] This is a difficulty that must be addressed directly. If Deleuze is utilising a Kantian perspective at the very foundation of his theory of subject formation, the question must be posed of whether this condemns his philosophical project to the same failures that he and many others have diagnosed in Kant. The answer to this question will have a significant impact on any project that attempts to build on Deleuzian insights.

Recent years have seen a growing awareness of the depth of Deleuze's debt to the Kantian perspective. Joe Hughes, for one, identifies a conceptual 'monotony' throughout Deleuze's work (including the work done with Guattari) that centres on a structure of synthesis as self-transcendence derived from Kant.[2] Hughes offers a breathtakingly comprehensive reading of Deleuze's oeuvre that takes seriously the latter's claim, in his 1994 'Preface to the English Edition' of *Difference and Repetition*, that the significance of that book for his later work lies in its Kantian legacy. In this Preface, written only two years before his death, Deleuze emphasises the importance of the theory of faculties, of error and the critique of common sense as essential for introducing his and Guattari's 'rhizomatic thought' in the *Capitalism and Schizophrenia* volumes (DR xvii). He also reserves a special place for the practice of critique developed in *Difference and Repetition*, writing that 'as long as the critique has not been carried to the heart of [the dogmatic] image of thought it is difficult to conceive of thought as ... involving encounters which escape all recognition ... or as attaining that which tears thought from its natural torpor and notorious bad will, and forces us to think' (DR xvi). As early as 1997 Diane Beddoes argued that even though scholars operating with a 'molar or majoritarian interpretation' of Kant understand critique as 'welded to reason, law, the categorical imperative', Deleuze and Guattari's citation in *Anti-Oedipus* of Kleist's understanding of Kant as 'the pulveriser, demolishing predictability, progress and faith and leaving only irresolvable ambiguities' indicates a continuation in *Anti-Oedipus* of Kant's critical project.[3] She claims that while it is true that 'Kant is saturated with the language of trial and law ... the meticulous deployment of critique in *Anti-Oedipus*', and the use of time to fracture the subject, opens up the 'question of passive synthesis which provides the basic machinery of *Anti-Oedipus*'.[4] Beddoes goes so far as to suggest that 'if we read backwards from *Capitalism and Schizophrenia* a case can be made for the claim that Kant lurks in the background, everywhere'.[5]

In *Difference and Repetition*, Deleuze criticises Images of thought modelled on recognition because they base their 'supposed principle upon extrapolation from certain facts, particularly insignificant facts such as Recognition, everyday banality in person; as though thought should not seek its models among stranger and more compromising adventures' (DR 135). If thought should seek its models among 'stranger' adventures than recognition, whose model should it use? Deleuze answers: 'take the example of Kant: of all philosophers, Kant is the one who discovers the prodigious domain of the transcendental' (DR 135). What Deleuze is suggesting is to replace the model of recognition, which was determined to represent all thought by extrapolation from banal empirical observations, with a 'stranger and more compromising' model based on Kant's transcendental analysis. In *Kant's Critical Philosophy*, the discovery and analysis of the transcendental is the function of critique. It is clear that in his early work Deleuze sees a valuable tool for the discovery of thought without Image in the model Kantian critique provides. But Deleuze does not just mean 'critique' in the vague sense of any evaluative analysis. When he proposes Kant's discovery of 'the prodigious domain of the transcendental' as the model for the discovery of a thought without Image he is advocating a return to Kantian critique understood as an examination of the structure and limitations of the faculties (DR 135). Deleuze believes such a critique can reveal the real interplay of powers beneath the dogmatic Image's presupposed unity of the subject and that in so doing the dogmatic Image can be resisted and thought freed from the necessity of forming a new Image. Not only is the critique a valuable tool for the discovery of a thought without Image through its analysis of the faculties, it is also a valuable tool in the creation of such a thought.

The first step in developing an appreciation of this trajectory in Deleuze's thought is to outline the features of the theory of faculties he develops in his early work. In *Difference and Repetition*, he adopts both the structure and logic of the doctrine of faculties he attributed to Kant five years earlier in *Kant's Critical Philosophy* and applied to his reading of Proust in 1964's *Proust and Signs*. This adoption did not happen without Deleuze making modifications. What is interesting about these modifications is that for the most part Deleuze did not treat them as a break from Kant's critical project but as a profound fidelity to that project. Though Deleuze repeatedly indicts Kant's critique, in the background of this indictment is the faith that critique can be recuperated, as he believes it was in the work of both Maïmon and Nietzsche. In *Nietzsche and Philosophy* and in *Difference and Repetition*, Deleuze makes the case that the critical project can become 'total' (NP 1) or be radically transformed (NP 52, DR 132) rather than simply abandoned (DR 153, 173). In many

The Theory of Faculties

ways *Difference and Repetition* can be seen as more loyal to the immanent project of critique than Kant's three Critiques were. This loyalty can be appreciated in the way the theory of faculties that critique identifies plays out. From the structural similarities and differences between the accounts of the movement from the experience of powerlessness to the 'beyond', to the parallel notions of sublimity and encounter, the accounts of the transcendental forms of the faculties, and the parallel notions of 'discordant harmony' and 'discordant accord', the consistency of Deleuze's prioritisation of the evaluation of limits in the move 'beyond' is evidence of the centrality of critique for this move.

The Differential Theory of Faculties

The critical analysis of faculties reveals the constituting forces of common sense that make the dogmatic Image of thought 'dogmatic'. In *Kant's Critical Philosophy* Deleuze develops a theory of the 'common doctrine of faculties' that he then modifies and applies in *Proust and Signs*, only to thematise and develop it further into what he calls the 'differential theory of faculties' in *Difference and Repetition* (DR vii). According to the 'common' doctrine of faculties, Kant's 'faculties of mind' legislate for the proper organisations of imagination, understanding and Reason. Whether the organisation legislated for is logical common sense or moral common sense depends on which faculty of mind is being exercised. In contrast, Deleuze's 'differential theory of faculties' eschews models that legislate from the outside or that break in any way with the immanent perspective. Yet this does not produce as sharp a break between the two accounts of faculties as one might suppose. Though Deleuze takes up only the second sense of 'faculty' he attributes to Kant in *Kant's Critical Philosophy*, he nonetheless uses Kant's model of the third 'faculty of mind' (the faculty of the feeling of pleasure and pain) for the logic of the genesis of the higher form of each faculty. Deleuze does this because the faculty of the feeling of pleasure and pain is the only faculty of mind that does not legislate the organisation of faculties but allows the faculties to spontaneously achieve their own organisation (KCP 48; DR 146). This is because for Kant the higher form of the faculty of the feeling of pleasure and pain is not *autonomous* but *heautonomous*. It legislates over itself rather than over the other active faculties or over either phenomena or noumena. On Deleuze's reading, by the time he writes the *Critique of Judgement* Kant realises that any organisation of faculties determined by common sense presupposes that the faculties are capable of a 'free and indeterminate' accord that is not pre-established by common sense but rather *creates* common sense (KCP 24; CJ §21–2). It is this model that Deleuze adopts as his own in *Difference and Repetition*.

Deleuze is clear in that work that he does not intend to produce another 'doctrine of the faculties' despite his attestation that such a doctrine is 'an entirely necessary component of the system of philosophy' (DR 143). All Deleuze claims to be doing is determining 'the nature of its requirements' (DR 144). What he outlines as 'requirements' for such a doctrine are found in the 'differential theory of faculties'. The difference between a 'doctrine' and a 'theory' is the typical one: while a doctrine is taken as complete and unassailable once accepted, a theory, as an hypothesis that owes its acceptance or rejection to continual experimentation and observation, is open to revision. Deleuze insists on this in order to emphasise that the particular list of faculties he isolates (sensibility, memory, imagination and thought) may not be comprehensive. In keeping with his commitment to avoid tracing the transcendental from the empirical, he must not judge the outcome of research before the research is done.[6] Unlike Deleuze's Kant, for whom the list of faculties is limited to the three or four types of representations for which they are the source, Deleuze's own list of faculties is potentially infinite given that for him faculties number as many as there are powers or capacities. It should be clear how much the language Deleuze uses to describe faculties resonates with the language he and Guattari use in *Capitalism and Schizophrenia* to describe desiring-machines, which are not individual things, but assemblages 'at work everywhere, functioning' (AO 1) as a system of 'interruptions or breaks' (AO 36), producing the subject as a residuum, and themselves subject to three passive syntheses: connective, disjunctive and conjunctive.[7] As Deleuze and Guattari write in *Anti-Oedipus*, 'drives are simply the desiring-machines themselves' (AO 35). Since there may be an infinite number of drives, powers, functions, or ways of relating – especially if the future is considered open to generating more ways of relating – it is not impossible that there are an infinite number of faculties. In addition to the faculties of sensibility, memory, imagination and thinking, Deleuze mentions faculties of stupidity, vitality and sociability, amongst others (DR 143, 159). But while there may be an infinite number of faculties, only faculties capable of attaining their own unique exercise – their superior or transcendental form –

The Theory of Faculties

have a place in Deleuze's differential theory of faculties. That is why the faculty of understanding that was so important in the 'common' doctrine of faculties is lost in the differential theory of faculties. From Deleuze's perspective, understanding does not have a transcendental exercise. This is because its function of concept formation depends on the faculty of sensibility, which means there is nothing that can *only* be conceived (apart from what is properly the object of imagination, not understanding). However, while the faculty of Reason is not referred to by name in *Difference and Repetition*, unlike understanding, Reason does not entirely disappear. Rather, Deleuze converts it into the faculty of thought. In *Kant's Critical Philosophy*, Reason is dangerous because it encourages the understanding to exceed its limits by enticing it with 'the illusion of a positive domain to conquer outside experience' (KCP 25). Yet, Deleuze argues that Kant's critical philosophy is organised around the faculty of Reason. This is because, as Kant himself points out in his *Groundwork of the Metaphysics of Morals* (1785), the mystery of why humans have Reason reveals a practical purpose of Nature.[8] Despite its danger, Reason holds out the promise of taking knowledge beyond the empirical sphere to grasp the 'unconditioned' – if only its interests can be properly hierarchised and the powers expressed by the other faculties be properly organised and limited. In Deleuze, the faculty of thought expresses the same kind of power (and danger) as Reason, but differently interpreted.

Like Kant's faculty of Reason, Deleuze's faculty of thought fundamentally poses a danger to knowledge (DR 135–6). Thought expresses the power of newness, of creativity, of contestation and of destruction, though in *Difference and Repetition*, unlike in *Kant's Critical Philosophy*, Deleuze insists that these powers of thought are imposed on and awakened in thought by the outside force of 'encounters' (DR 139). For Deleuze, the mystery of why humans have thought reveals the power of Difference itself – which is not a transcendent 'beyond' but an immanent 'beneath' (DR 214). Thought, again like the faculty of Reason in *Kant's Critical Philosophy*, produces Ideas that resist categorisation and representation according to knowledge (DR 146–7). For Deleuze, this resistance to representation/categorisation helps thought to form new problematic fields for questioning. And though it is not the only faculty capable of producing Ideas, thought has a 'special relationship' to Ideas such that it must be understood in its highest form as the expression or actualisation of Ideas (DR 194). Thought thus holds out the promise of breaking with *doxa* by internalising the power of Difference instantiated in the encounter and producing a thought without Image – but only if the other faculties realise their highest internal power through the serial transmission from one to the other of the violence of the encounter with Difference that forces them to confront and transcend their limits.

The accounts given in *Difference and Repetition* and *Kant's Critical Philosophy* of how faculties achieve their 'higher', 'superior' or 'transcendent' forms are remarkably similar. For both Kant and Deleuze, a faculty's lower form corresponds to its empirical exercise, while its higher form corresponds to its transcendent exercise (DR 142). In *Kant's Critical Philosophy*, it is the faculties of mind that are capable of both a higher and a lower form. In their lower form, the relation expressed by the faculties is one of dependency. In their higher form, however, the faculties of mind become autonomous. For Deleuze's Kant, a faculty becomes autonomous when it 'finds *in itself* the law of its own exercise' rather than taking it from something external (KCP 4). In other words, when the faculty legislates over itself. In *Difference and Repetition*, in its lower form the faculty grasps what other faculties can grasp: it is subject to the model of recognition. In its higher or transcendental form it grasps what it alone is capable of grasping (DR 140). The superior or transcendent form of a faculty is characterised by Deleuze as the moment when the faculty grasps that in the world which concerns it exclusively (what can *only* be sensed, imagined, remembered or thought), in other words, its radical difference or specificity. Thus, according to both accounts, the lower form is characterised by dependency: in *Kant's Critical Philosophy* it is dependency on empirical content while in *Difference and Repetition* it is dependency on the model of recognition (which is ultimately empirically derived as well). At the level of the higher form, the picture gets a little more complicated. The notion of 'autonomy' in *Kant's Critical Philosophy* becomes the notion of 'singularity' in *Difference and Repetition*. Like 'autonomy', 'singularity' is attained by submission to the law – but it is a submission that is self-generated and reveals what is most unique. As Deleuze writes in the context of describing relations to the law that exemplify both contestation and resignation:

> Job is infinite contestation and Abraham infinite resignation, but these are one and the same thing. Job challenges the law in an ironic manner, refusing all second-hand explanations and dismissing the general in order to reach the most singular as principle or as universal. Abraham submits

humorously to the law, but finds in that submission precisely the singularity of his only son whom the law commanded him to sacrifice. (DR 7)

From Deleuze's perspective, Job's challenge to the law and Abraham's submission to it are the same thing. Both reveal and create singularity in so far as they are critical attitudes that question limits in order to produce a relationship to those limits that acknowledges the impossibility of getting beyond the limits and thereby operates at the limit. For all Job's contestation, he is still subject to the law and comes to understand and will the law. For Abraham, his willingness to submit to the law allows the law to release him and give him back his son. As with Kant's notion of freedom as submission to the power of the moral law within oneself, the notion of singularity as self-giving of the law combines in tense union a way of being that is both within the law and beyond it. This is repeated in *Kant's Critical Philosophy* when the higher form is autonomous in so far as its finds its law within itself, while in *Difference and Repetition* the higher form is singular in so far as it discovers its own specificity by submission to its own internal law or principle, which Deleuze usually expresses by saying that it grasps what it *alone* is capable of grasping. Moreover, the higher form in both accounts is formal rather than empirical.[9]

Of course, by calling the higher form of a faculty 'transcendent', in *Difference and Repetition*, Deleuze does not mean to suggest that the faculty grasps something outside the world, 'but, on the contrary, that it grasps that in the world which concerns it exclusively and brings it into the world': Difference (DR 143). It is their grasping of their own difference, precisely at the limit of what they *can* do, that is the key to the faculties' transcendent exercises in both *Kant's Critical Philosophy* and *Difference and Repetition*. When imagination is forced to its limit by the experience of the sublime it transcends that limit (negatively) as it internalises what appears to be an external limitation, thereby discovering its own hidden power and highest form. When faculties grasp their own difference they are grasping their limit (understood as their highest power), and their transcendent exercise entails not going beyond existence but grasping that which makes them exist in their specificity or essence. Both *Difference and Repetition*'s transcendental empiricism and *Kant's Critical Philosophy*'s critique identify the 'transcendental' form of each faculty and how it is achieved. But another way of putting this would be to describe Deleuze's overarching approach as identifying each faculty's limits. The limit is the primary concept both *Difference and Repetition* and *Kant's Critical Philosophy* utilise to describe each faculties' achievement of its transcendent exercise. A faculty achieves its higher, transcendent exercise when it is confronted with its own limit through an experience of encounter or sublimity. Each transcendental form designates the faculty's powerlessness/limit at the empirical or impure level and simultaneously its power/limit of 'transcending' that empirical exercise to achieve its formal (or pure) exercise.

Sensibility

The serial movement by which each faculty achieves its transcendent exercise begins in sensibility. Of course, both *Kant's Critical Philosophy* and *Difference and Repetition* locate sensibility at the origin of all facultative relations, yet what Deleuze means by sensibility in the latter work differs from what he means by it in the former. In *Difference and Repetition*, sensibility is not equivalent with everyday empirical experiences. The empirical is already representational – hence it is always necessarily predetermined by *doxa* since it is 'given' under the form of common sense. 'Sensations' in *Difference and Repetition* are 'sub-representative' and immediate affects (DR 57). Like Kant's manifold of intuition, Deleuze's 'sensations' are intuitive yet undergo their own 'passive syntheses' before relating with the active syntheses that make up representational experience and thought (DR 71–5). The comparison is between Deleuze's 'passive syntheses' in *Difference and Repetition* and *Anti-Oedipus* and what Kant calls the a priori manifold of the forms of sensibility (space and time) in the *Critique of Pure Reason* (CPR A77/B102). Unlike Kant's manifold of intuition, the passive syntheses constitutive of Deleuze's 'sensations' in *Difference and Repetition* are not the forms of space and time but the 'contractions' of habit derived from Hume that 'are not carried out *by* the mind, but happen *in* the mind' (DR 71). Sensibility is an unconscious process, yet, as Dan Smith has argued, for Deleuze, 'sensibility itself is intelligible'.[10] What Smith means is that for Deleuze sensibility is not a pure intuition in Kant's sense. Sensibility is genuinely produced in the passive syntheses, allowing *Difference and Repetition* to conceive of it not simply on the basis of receptivity, but as spontaneous, productive and creative. It is this sense of passivity that is taken up in *Anti-Oedipus*'s theory of desire: 'Desire is the set of *passive syntheses* that engineer partial objects, flows, and bodies, and that function as units of production . . . the auto-production of the unconscious' (AO 26). It is at the level of these passive syntheses that the question of the preparatory education of sensibility for the experience of encounter must take place.

Before moving to the analysis of the encounter, it should be noted that this difference between how Deleuze conceives of sensibility in *Difference and Repetition* and how he reads Kant's conception of sensibility in *Kant's Critical Philosophy* illuminates something important for understanding the general project of the later work. Whereas in *Kant's Critical Philosophy* the transcendental method moves past empiricism by focusing on the *forms* of experience rather than experience itself, Deleuze thinks that transcendental philosophy must go beyond the *conditioning* method of identifying forms to achieve a *genesis* of experience and, ultimately, of real thought beyond experience. While *Kant's Critical Philosophy* holds that certain ideal and universal structures of the mind must be operating as conditions in order for there to be experience, the suggestion in *Difference and Repetition* that sensibility is productive and intelligible shifts the analysis to the genesis of receptivity, experience and thought from Difference itself. This critical emphasis on immanence eliminates the problem of extrinsicism and heralds the importance Deleuze's critique of the faculties has for developing an ethics that relies not on principles but – like virtue ethics – on the formation of character.

Encounter

Everyday acts of recognition result from the harmony of the faculties working under the legislation of common sense, which Deleuze refers to as the 'natural exercise' of the faculties (DR 131). By way of contrast, real thought is necessarily 'involuntary', 'constrained' and 'born, illegitimately, of fortuitousness in the world' (DR 139). It is with a touch of irony that Deleuze reminds his readers that '"Everybody" knows very well that in fact men think rarely, and more often under the impulse of a shock than in the excitement of a taste for thinking' (DR 132). For Deleuze, real thought is not an everyday occurrence nor is it the result of a decision or a desire – it is the result of a 'shock'. Real thought needs such a shock in order to awaken it from the dogmatic 'natural stupor' it finds itself living out under the form of common sense (DR 139). The sort of shock that has the power to awaken thought could only come via the sensation of Difference itself as the 'original violence inflicted upon thought' (DR 139).[11] While some sensations are taken up in active syntheses to form representations, there are others that bear within themselves their origin in Difference and have the power to contest representation itself. These are what Deleuze calls 'encounters' (DR 165). Deleuze reserves this word 'encounter' for the forms of Difference that transmit a 'shock' or 'violence' from sensibility to thought. The encounter opposes all recognition (DR 142), and the only way to spark real thought is through an encounter. In Deleuze's words:

> Something in the world forces us to think. This something is an object not of recognition but of a fundamental *encounter*. What is encountered may be Socrates, a temple or a demon. It may be grasped in a range of affective tones: wonder, love, hatred, suffering. In whichever tone, its primary characteristic is that it can only be sensed. (DR 139)

It is tempting to say that the encounter could be anything that forces a problematising of one's habits of thought: Descartes' meditations, Hume's scepticism, a chair mounted upside down on a wall, a painting of a pipe that declares 'This is not a pipe', even a bit of gift wrap crumpled in a corner or an anthropomorphised red balloon. But there is at least one parameter Deleuze sets for encounters: they all emerge from sensibility. Indeed, encounters are the purest form of sensibility in so far as they can 'only be sensed'. More accurately, the encounter is the form in which sensibility senses 'what can only be sensed' (DR 57):

> The privilege of sensibility as origin appears in the fact that, in an encounter, what forces sensation and that which can only be sensed are one and the same thing, whereas in other cases the two instances are distinct. In effect, the intensive or difference in intensity is at once both the object of the encounter and the object to which the encounter raises sensibility. (DR 144–5)

The encounter is the vehicle for the sensation of Difference but it is also the very sensation that it is meant to produce. In other words, the encounter produces itself in its sensation. It is able to do this because the encounter is not 'given' under the form of common sense like most experience is. This is the meaning behind Deleuze's formula that it is what can *only* be sensed. The encounter is not available to memory or imagination or thought, so it cannot be recognised since recognition requires unification of the object through all of the faculties. What can *only* be sensed, what Deleuze elsewhere refers to as 'the *sentiendum*', is 'the paradoxical existence of a "something" which simultaneously cannot be sensed from the point of view of the empirical exercise) and can only be sensed (from the point of view of the transcendent exercise)' of the faculty of sensibility. (DR 236)

The encounter's paradoxical nature comes from its simultaneous impossibility and necessity at the level of sensation. The encounter forces sensibility to the point of the breakdown of its empirical exercise – but it is precisely at that point that sensibility achieves its 'transcendent' exercise. This point of breakdown is both the point of the faculty's powerlessness and its greatest power. To understand this, take as an example the experience of encountering certain demanding pieces of art, for instance the painting *Blue Monochrome* (1961) by Yves Klein.[12] Klein's blue is sharp, ultra-saturated, jarring, even violent. It is a kind of electric blue that pulsates with its own energy. It is blue, but it is not blue. It is different from any other blue. The immediate sensation of it is unexpected, insistent and utterly unrepresentable. This description is merely the shadow of an echo of the piece itself.[13] Indeed, without the piece being immediately in sight it is impossible to quite remember the exact quality of the blue or even imagine it in its fullness. The New York Museum of Modern Art's gallery label for the piece suggests the viewer recognise in it the artist's intention to produce a utopian vision of 'an open window to freedom'. However, as interesting as that is, it fails to capture the immediate sensation of the piece itself. The blue of *Blue Monochrome* cannot be appreciated from the point of view of the ordinary empirical use (or 'exercise') of the senses. The ordinary empirical use of the senses requires recognisability and as such would experience the painting as just another shade of bright blue. But the power of the piece is that it does not allow the ordinary empirical use of the senses to determine it. The blue of *Blue Monochrome* makes the viewer stop and pay attention. It is a sensation that forces the experience of the blue's singularity and power at the 'transcendental' level where the senses perceive in this 'blue' the intensive dimension of blueness. In Deleuze's vocabulary, the encounter with Klein's painting forces the sensation of Difference itself as the internal genetic power responsible for its unique blueness. Of course, the encounter could be with Klein's *Blue Monochrome*, Kundera's analysis of the gesture in *Immortality*, the first three chords of Wagner's *Tristan und Isolde*, or any number of other experiences that resist recognition according to the common sense use of the faculties. The important thing is that at the level of sensation the encounter resists recognisability through a singularity and power that forces sensation beyond the empirical to the transcendental.

Echoes of Kantianism are easily visible in this description. What *Difference and Repetition* calls an 'encounter' and what *Kant's Critical Philosophy* calls the 'sublime' are remarkably similar.[14] Both emerge from sensibility to produce a 'shock' or 'violence' that confronts the faculties with their limits. In Kant's *Critique of Judgement*, the sublime is the experience of being faced with either formlessness or deformity in nature (the immensity of 'the wide ocean, enraged by storms' and the power of Nature 'in its wildest and most unruly disorder and devastation' (CJ §23)). Deleuze writes that for Kant the experience of sublimity 'is as if the imagination were confronted with its own limit, forced to strain to its utmost, experiencing a violence which stretches it to the extremity of its power' (KCP 50). The sublime is an experience of deformity that forces the imagination violently to the very limit of its power, and even beyond it – at least negatively. From *Difference and Repetition*'s point of view, the sort of shock that has the power to awaken the faculties to their highest power could only come from the 'original violence' (DR 139) of a sensation that has the power to contest representation itself. Encounters are the sensations that have that power. Thus the encounter transmits its shock or 'violence' from sensibility to thought by opposing all recognition (DR 142). Moreover, the only way real thought can begin is through an encounter. To borrow from Kant's vocabulary, Deleuze's notion of the encounter might be thought of as a 'form' of real thought. On every important point of description – their origin, their power, their object and their violence – the 'sublime' and the 'encounter' echo one another.

However, Deleuze's insistence in *Difference and Repetition* that the encounter can only be generated from sensibility leads to a point of potential divergence between the theories of encounter and sublimity. In *Kant's Critical Philosophy* Deleuze is careful to clarify that for Kant, while it may seem at first that imagination experiences the inadequacy of its power when faced with sublimity in Nature itself, it is actually Reason that forces the imagination to attempt to comprehend the immensity and power of Nature. It is not Nature, but Reason's Ideas posed as problems or limits beyond the possibility of experience that push imagination to the limit of its power, 'forcing it to admit that all its power is nothing in comparison to an Idea' (KCP 51). If Deleuze is right to say that the experience of the sublime comes from Ideas and not really from Nature, the encounter and the sublime are not entirely equivalent notions. After all, in *Kant's Critical Philosophy* the experience of the sublime is generated from Reason's imposition of Ideas that exceed the imagination's power, while in *Difference and Repetition* the encounter is produced from certain types of experience that strike sensibility as a shock. However, Deleuze's account of Ideas as 'questions' overcomes this apparent divergence. For Deleuze, 'questions' are problematic Ideas in their function of forcing faculties into their transcendent exercise. In the example of Klein's *Blue Monochrome*, 'questions' are produced in the experience of being struck by the blueness of the painting. Questions such as 'How is this *blue* so different?', 'How did this blue become so intense?', 'Why can I not look away?', 'Where did this blue come from?' or 'How many other colours have never been discovered or experienced?' These questions and others 'furnish the conditions under which the faculties attain their superior exercise' (DR 146). The experience of asking these questions in front of *Blue Monochrome* forces the experience of the blue's uniqueness and power – and this is what forces sensibility to its higher exercise in sensing the intensity of the blueness that would have been insensible from the lower empirical use of the faculty. In *Kant's Critical Philosophy*, Deleuze explains that it is not the experience of the sublime but the Idea that forces imagination to confront its limit. In the sense that 'encounter' and (the form of Idea as) 'question' are equivalent in Deleuze's differential theory of faculties, it draws his account of the encounter closer to the account of sublimity *Kant's Critical Philosophy*, since they can both be understood as generated from the experience of Ideas. This is a crucial point of overlap between the Deleuzian and Kantian registers for at least three reasons: the potential Kantian contamination that still waits to be addressed; the power of the active practice of critique to have a transformative impact at the level of the passive syntheses; and the reconceptualisation of the idea of the limit that Deleuze's work in *Difference and Repetition* produces.

Limit

Deleuze deems it no less than the 'essential thesis' of the critical method that Reason's ends *'differ in nature'* and 'form an organic and hierarchical system' (KCP 7/13). What is implied in the claim that Reason's ends differ in nature (that is, in kind rather than merely in degree[15]) is that attention to differences is fundamental to the critically immanent perspective. A truly immanent account of Reason's ends must differentiate what is within Reason's bounds from what is beyond them. Another way of putting this would be to describe the critique through its function of identifying Reason's limits. Deleuze points out that immanent critique condemns not only Reason's attempts to exceed its limits but also its failure to reach its limits:

> The so-called transcendental method is always the determination of an *immanent* employment of Reason, conforming to one of its interests. The *Critique of Pure Reason* thus *condemns* the transcendent employment of a speculative Reason which claims to legislate by itself; the *Critique of Practical Reason condemns* the transcendent employment of a practical Reason which, instead of legislating by itself, lets itself be empirically conditioned (CPrR Introduction). (KCP 36–7/54)

Critique attempts to identify Reason's immanent or intrinsic power in relation to each of its ends so as to enforce its legitimate employment. This means critique attempts to ensure Reason reaches the limit of its power without going beyond that limit. This is a subtle shift in the way Deleuze reads limitation: no longer in terms of merely imposing a maximum by which to rein in Reason's ambition, but in terms of identifying the full extent of a faculty's power.[16] Of course, when Reason's limit is exceeded in relation to its speculative end, it succumbs to the illusion that it possesses knowledge it could not possibly have: knowledge of God, the soul and freedom. Critique cannot prevent the formation of these illusions but only their harmful consequences. If Reason is limited to its own realm and not allowed to attempt to legislate over the phenomena of experience, its danger is contained. The critical act of limitation then frees Reason to pursue its legitimate employment to the fullest. For example, Reason is entirely justified in adopting certain 'regulative' principles concerning the ultimate basis of human experience. As explained above, for the purposes of knowledge Reason's legitimate use is to pose the Idea of systematic unity in Nature 'as a problem or a limit' (KCP 20), an ideal focal point outside experience 'towards which the concepts of the understanding converge' (KCP 19). This Idea of systematic unity in Nature must be an a priori principle because it is never given in experience, even in many experiences taken together. Thus the Idea is merely presupposed in order to confer on the concepts of the understanding laws that ensure their maximal completeness and systematicity. While it is unknown whether Nature actually is law-like, the principle that such unity is possible and thus worthy of being sought forms a *regulative principle* of Reason. By contrast, the claim that such unity *does* exist would represent a 'constitutive'

The Theory of Faculties

principle, which is the sort of knowledge claim that cannot be critically justified.

What this description is meant to illustrate is that critique is not just interested in disciplining the faculties when they exceed their limits – it is also interested in the faculties realising their power up to their limits. And while the higher form of pleasure in judgements of beauty requires imagination and understanding, there is another type of aesthetic experience – one that expresses a higher form of pain – that explicitly links Reason's power of limitation with the realisation of imagination's full power. A critique of the genesis of aesthetic common sense begins in that type of experience – the experience of the sublime.

The notion of the limit is thus another parallel between *Kant's Critical Philosophy* and *Difference and Repetition*. In his reading of Kant, Deleuze emphasises how critique attempts to identify Reason's power in relation to each of its ends so as to enforce its legitimate employment. This means that critique attempts to ensure Reason reaches the limit of its power without going beyond that limit. This is a subtle shift in the way Deleuze reads limitation: no longer in terms of merely imposing a maximum by which to rein in Reason's ambition, but in terms of identifying the full extent of a faculty's power. Deleuze's analyses of power proceed through an analysis of what a thing 'can do', or a thing's potential. Deleuze believes that a thing's potential can be evaluated by evaluating its capacity to achieve and transcend its limits. In *Difference and Repetition*, just like in *Kant's Critical Philosophy*, limitation is no longer conceived in terms of merely imposing a principle of measurement or a maximum by which to rein in a faculty's power, but in terms of identifying the full extent of its power and the basis on which that power is deployed to its fullest. In this new sense, limitation refers to the intrinsic power of a thing or faculty (DR 201). It is this sense of limitation that Deleuze and Guattari transform into the concept of production in *Anti-Oedipus*, with the process of deterritorialisation replacing that of the evaluation of a faculty's full power.

Anti-Oedipus begins with a preface written by Michel Foucault in which he not only claims that the book is 'the first book of ethics to be written in France in quite a long time' (AO xiii) but also articulates a number of 'essential principles' that can be derived from it. The third of these principles is to 'withdraw allegiance from the old categories of the Negative (law, limit, castration, lack, lacuna)' (AO xviii). Deleuze criticises the notion of the limit in *Anti-Oedipus* as well as in *Difference and Repetition*. However, the positive productive notion of the limit he is attempting to articulate in his earlier works is crucial for appreciating the model of production developed later with Guattari.

While there are several places in *Difference and Repetition* where Deleuze criticises the concept of the limit, there are also places where he suggests a revised understanding of the limit in terms of the intrinsic power of a faculty. In the very first chapter of the book, he defines limitation as 'a type of distribution that divides up the distributed according to the rules of analogy determined by common sense' (DR 36). This understanding of limitation as a way of organising beings according to a pre-given principle established by common sense is in contrast with 'nomadism' understood as a type of distribution that happens according to 'a division among those who distribute *themselves* in an open space – a space which is unlimited, or at least without precise limits' (DR 36). As an example, consider two different ways of organising buttons: one way would be to separate them by size into the different compartments of a sewing box, then if a certain size button is needed, it is just a matter of looking in the designated compartment. This is the method recommended by common sense. Another way would be to put all the buttons in one big glass jar. If a small button is needed, look at the bottom of the jar. If a big button is needed, look at the top of the jar. This method relies on the buttons distributing themselves – the smaller falling to the bottom and the bigger getting pushed to the top. Deleuze repeats this distinction between ways of organising with regard to different types of hierarchy: a hierarchy of limits that measures beings according to a principle, and an 'ontological' hierarchy that measures beings according to their power (DR 37). The distinction in both instances is between a form of organisation of beings that proceeds according to a pre-given principle and one that proceeds according to the powers and problems internal to the beings themselves. In both instances the notion of the limit is used to describe the organisation of beings that proceeds according to a pre-given principle. Deleuze connects the notion of limitation with the notions of resemblance (DR 12), representation (DR 43), negativity (DR 112), common sense (DR 140) and opposition (DR 266), all terms Deleuze ties to the dogmatic Image of thought.[17] Moreover, as often as Deleuze criticises the notion of the limit he honours that of the *un*limited (DR 36, 57, 141). However, there is another way of understanding the notion of the limit present in Deleuze's thought, one that is fundamental to

The Theory of Faculties

an understanding of his differential theory of faculties as well as the ethics derivable from it.

After introducing the distinction between organisations that happen according to an external principle and organisations that happen according to each member's intrinsic power, Deleuze goes on to explain that for organisations based on power,

> it is not a question of considering absolute degrees of power, but only of knowing whether a being eventually 'leaps over' or transcends its limits in going to the limit of what it can do, whatever its degree. 'To the limit', it will be argued, still presupposes a limit. Here, limit [*peras*] no longer refers to what maintains the thing under a law, nor to what delimits or separates it from other things. On the contrary, it refers to that on the basis of which it [the thing] is deployed and deploys all its power; ... *the smallest becomes equivalent to the largest* once it is not separated from what it can do. (DR 37)

Seemingly incongruously based on his repeated uses of the notion of limitation as an activity determined by recognition and common sense, Deleuze claims that the analysis of power proceeds according to an evaluation of limits. However, he does not think that by utilising the notion of limit he is making the mistake of smuggling in the idea of a pre-given principle he meant to avoid when he criticised the notion of limit. The analysis of power does not proceed according to the principle of pre-given degrees of power – it proceeds through an analysis of what a thing can do, or, a body's power. Deleuze believes that a thing's power can be evaluated by evaluating its capacity to achieve and transcend its limits. Limitation is thus no longer understood in terms of merely imposing a principle of measurement or a maximum by which to rein in the faculty's power, but in terms of identifying the full extent of a faculty's power and the basis on which its power is deployed to its fullest. In this new sense, limitation is not teleological. Rather, it refers to the intrinsic power of a thing or faculty (DR 201).[18]

There are thus two notions of the limit operating in Deleuze's work. One that is inextricably tied to the dogmatic Image of thought and another that 'refers to that on the basis of which it [a thing] is deployed and deploys all its power' (DR 37). Deleuze himself acknowledges that the 'significance of the very notion of limit changes completely' when he writes that the notion of limit 'no longer refers to the limits of finite representation' but 'to the womb in which finite determination never ceases to be born and to disappear' (DR 43).

When he discusses limitation in the new terms of the basis on which a thing is deployed and deploys all its power, he means to associate the limit with the origin of things – that is, the origin of empirical experiences and thought – in Difference itself. The limit is the point at which things dissolve into and are born again from Difference, which does not distinguish forms (as would be the object for the method of conditioning) but the genesis of a thing out of Difference itself. From this perspective, things are empirical manifestations of Difference's power of genesis. It is at the level of faculties that Deleuze thinks it is possible to analyse those powers so as to understand the genesis of a thought without Image.

When it comes to the theory of faculties, the limit is the primary concept Deleuze utilises to describe each faculties' achievement of its transcendent exercise. A faculty achieves its superior, transcendent exercise when it is confronted with its own limit through an encounter with Difference itself. Deleuze writes:

> What is most important, however, is that – between sensibility and imagination, between imagination and memory, between memory and thought – when each disjointed faculty communicates to another the violence which carries it to its own limit, every time it is a free form of difference which awakens the faculty, and awakens it as the different within that difference. (DR 145)

It is the violence of Difference as instantiated in the experience of the encounter that forces each faculty in turn to its limit or transcendent exercise. In its lower or empirical form, the faculty grasps what other faculties can grasp: it is subject to the model of recognition. It experiences the same 'blue' in the sky, in the couch, and in *Blue Monochrome* – that is, a 'blue' that can be simultaneously sensed, remembered, imagined and conceived. In its higher or transcendental form the faculty grasps what it alone is capable of grasping (DR 140). Sensation senses the particular, incomparable, and (from the point of view of the empirical exercise of sensibility) insensible blueness of *Blue Monochrome*; imagination produces the image of that which is unimaginable – the image of pure freedom from the formless and unique intensity of Klein's new blue; memory remembers the immemorial – the recollection of a genius and creativity that never happened but is nonetheless remembered and thereby becomes enmeshed in our unconscious passive syntheses; and thought thinks the unthinkable – the thought of uniqueness, freedom and creation that is *not* unique, free or new from the point of view of the empirical use of thought. From the empirical point of view, such a thought is nonsense. From the transcendental point of view, however, such a thought is real in so far as it connects thinking with Difference itself and the internal powers and problems at the root of the genesis of *Blue Monochrome* and of its power to produce the experience of intensity, the image of freedom, the memory of creation and the thought of the paradoxical impossibility and necessity of each. To anticipate where this movement is headed: it is by internalising their powerlessness at the empirical level that the faculties achieve their greatest power at the transcendental level. As is well known, *Anti-Oedipus* problematises this concept of internalisation as it is tied so closely to the historical language of psychoanalysis. However, the desiring-machine's production through the three passive syntheses recreates this same model of the internalisation of limitation as the move from the 'transcendent' to the 'immanent' and legitimate use of the syntheses in 'rediscovering a transcendental unconscious' (AO 75). The real power of the unconscious is revealed through its passivity.

Power and limitation are inextricably linked in the logic of Deleuze's theory of faculties because power and powerlessness are inextricably bound together in the theory of faculties. At the level of faculties, what drives the movement from sensibility to thought can be described in terms of either power *or* powerlessness. Deleuze associates powerlessness with 'real limits' early in *Difference and Repetition* (DR 13). Right at the origin of thought, in the passive syntheses of contraction and habit, Deleuze claims that there are powers inherent to sensibility but that these powers are unconscious and thus testify to our powerlessness as much as to our power. Moreover, the superior form of sensibility, the 'very being of the sensible' is revealed in 'what can *only* be sensed' (DR 57). What can only be sensed is the limit and powerlessness of sensibility from the point of view of its empirical exercise and the limit and the highest power of sensibility from the point of view of its transcendent exercise. Power and powerlessness refer to the same thing (as in the example of sensibility's relation to the blueness of Klein's *Blue Monochrome*), but reveal the faculty's power or its powerlessness depending on the point of view. Even the importance of violence in the encounter is conceived in terms of powerlessness. Under the influence of the encounter, faculties transmit their constraint (that is, their powerlessness) from one to the other. As Deleuze writes:

> Henceforth, thought is also forced to think its central collapse, its fracture, its own natural 'powerlessness' which is indistinguishable from the greatest power – in other words, from those unformulated forces, the *cogitanda*, as though from so many thefts or trespasses in thought. (DR 147)

In this passage Deleuze reconceives 'powerlessness' as the 'greatest power'. This is because it is the 'power' of the limit that in the case of each faculty connects that faculty with its superior exercise. The encounter plunges each faculty in its turn into an involuntary adventure in which it 'is borne to the extreme point of its dissolution' through a triple violence. First, there is the violence of the encounter that forces sensibility's exercise. Second there is the violence of grasping what that faculty alone can grasp. Third there is the violence of the ungraspable. Each faculty thus discovers its unique 'power' through its limit or powerlessness at the level of its empirical exercise. But it also discovers its difference and its repetition. For instance, the faculty of thought, when confronted with what it alone is capable of grasping, finds its difference. But when thought is confronted with what is unthinkable it instantaneously engenders the repetition of thinking. The faculty is able to separate and 'transcend' its lower, empirical exercise because of the violence of encountering its limit or powerlessness in the face of something that exceeds its empirical powers. In Deleuze's own words:

> Each faculty is unhinged, but what are the hinges if not the form of a common sense that causes all the faculties to function and converge? Each one, in its own order and on its own account, has broken the form of common sense which kept it within the empirical element of *doxa*, in order to attain both its 'nth' power and the paradoxical element within transcendental exercise. Rather than all the faculties converging and contributing to a common project of recognising an object, we see divergent projects in which, with regard to what concerns it essentially, each faculty is in the presence of that which is its 'own'. Discord of the faculties, chain of force and fuse along which each confronts its limit, receiving from (or communicating to) the other only a violence which brings it face to face with its own element, as though with its disappearance or its perfection. (DR 141)

Each transcendental form designates the faculty's *powerlessness* at the empirical level of common sense yet its *power* of transcending that empirical exercise to grasp its unique object. It is in this sense that powerlessness as instantiated by the limit is understood by Deleuze as the greatest power. The powerlessness of common sense thinking to grasp the unthinkable forces it to put into question and abandon common sense, which allows it to achieve its 'transcendent' form: a thought without Image. The 'internalization of powerlessness' refers precisely to this phenomenon. The forms in which this powerlessness comes to thought are 'imperatives in the form of questions . . . [that] point which designates "the impossibility of thinking that is thought", that point at which "powerlessness" is transmuted into power, that point which develops in the work in the form of a problem' (DR 199). The thought without Image that emerges is supposed to be thought freed from the form of common sense, otherwise known as a 'problem'. It is therefore puzzling that Deleuze associates its emergence with a 'discordant harmony' (DR 146). The language of harmony suggests that he may have inadvertently smuggled the form of common sense into his account of how the faculties free themselves from common sense – but the real story is much stranger.

Discordant Harmony

From the Kantian perspective, it is not Nature but Reason's Ideas posed as problems or limits beyond the possibility of experience that push imagination to the limit of its power, 'forcing it to admit that all its power is nothing in comparison to an Idea' (KCP 51). Imagination is powerless to reproduce Nature in its sublimity because of the Ideas Reason attaches to it (such as that of systematic unity). The relationship between Reason and imagination in the experience of the sublime is thus 'primarily a *dissention*' – a discord rather than an accord. But this discord gives rise to an accord. As Deleuze puts it, 'the pain makes a pleasure possible' (KCP 51). The experience of the sublime forces imagination to internalise its powerlessness, and this internalisation allows it to exceed the limits on its power 'in a negative fashion' (KCP 51). The awe and powerlessness felt in the sublime becomes an experience of the infinite in Nature. In this experience the imagination 'shakes loose' of its sensible bounds, seemingly exceeding its power – for no faculty is really capable of representing something beyond experience, which 'the infinite' certainly is. As such, this going beyond is merely negative. The 'presentation of the infinite' does not actually extend imagination's power to intuit things beyond experience. Imagination is simply reproducing its powerlessness – internally, then externally. The important thing about this is not just that it gives one more example of an illusion internal to the faculties. Deleuze goes on to claim that though the presentation of the infinite is only negative, the impression it makes on the imagination 'expands the soul',[19] which is then felt as 'the indeterminate suprasensible unity of all the faculties' (KCP 75, 51). Thus from the feeling of powerlessness we come to the unity of the faculties. This discordant accord is the critical genesis of aesthetic common sense, the discordant accord that the faculties spontaneously produce in the experience of the sublime.

Although Deleuze does not make the point explicitly, it is clear he understands Kant to be suggesting that the discordant accord of the faculties underlies the unity of the subject. According to Deleuze's reading, the Kantian subject is a locus of relations of faculties or drives. These faculties are not units – of possession or otherwise. They are capacities or powers that describe and are subject to variable relationships. So, according to Deleuze, the Kantian subject is a locus of shifting power relations. What guarantees that the discord amongst the faculties will produce an accord – that is, a unitary subject and stable objects – is not simply the unity of apperception required for knowledge but on a deeper level the 'soul' from which common sense arises. The choice of the word 'soul' here is significant. The French word '*l'âme*', like the English word 'soul', connotes a vital force of moral intelligence, associated with the breath. Kant's term for soul, '*Seele*', shares these connotations but must be distinguished from '*Geist*' or spirit (CJ §49 'On the faculties of the mind that constitute genius'). *Seele* is the totality of *all* psychic processes, i.e., it is a comprehensive term that Kant uses to describe an element containing all the faculties.[20] *Geist*, in contrast, is an 'animating principle' within the soul, which Kant defines as 'the capacity for representing a sublimity in objects' (CJ 'First Introduction: XII Division of the Critique of the Power of Judgement'). On this understanding, spirit is a faculty belonging within the soul. This distinction is important to bear in mind even though Deleuze does not make it explicit, because otherwise it is unclear from Deleuze's citations of Kant's work where he gets the idea of naming what unifies the faculties as 'the soul'. Without the distinction between spirit and soul, it would be tempting to interpret the 'expansion' of the soul as exclusively an 'elevation' above the 'tyranny of sensible tendencies' (CJ §83).

If this Kantian story is contrasted with the Deleuzian one, it is clear that the organisational parallel between the 'common' doctrine of the faculties and the differential theory is continued at the level of the (dis)unity of faculties. Deleuze's account of 'discordant harmony' in *Difference and Repetition* echoes that of the 'discordant accord'

The Theory of Faculties

he attributed to Kant five years earlier in *Kant's Critical Philosophy*. In *Kant's Critical Philosophy* the aesthetic common sense produced from the violent awakening of each faculty to its power is a 'discordant accord', whereas in *Difference and Repetition* the violence of the encounter with intensity is communicated from sensibility to imagination, from imagination to memory, and from memory to thought, producing a thought without Image that exists as a 'discordant harmony' (DR 146). This communication happens the way an epiphany happens: all of a sudden, completely, and through the inspiration created in one faculty sparking an inspiration in the next. And the medium of this communication is what Deleuze enigmatically refers to as the 'dark precursor' (DR 145). He introduces the term by writing that 'the dark precursor is sufficient to enable communication between difference as such, and to make the different communicate with difference: the dark precursor is not a friend' (DR 145). It is puzzling that after so carefully recreating the Kantian account of the genesis of aesthetic common sense Deleuze would rely on any assumed principle as a condition of the communication between faculties. However, he anticipates the objection that the dark precursor reintroduces the form of common sense:

> The very principle of communication, even if this should be violence, seems to maintain the form of a common sense. However, it is nothing of the sort. There is indeed a serial connection between the faculties and an order in that series. But neither the order nor the series implies any collaboration with regard to the form of a supposed same object or to a subjective unity in the nature of an 'I think'. It is a forced and broken connection which traverses the fragments of a dissolved self as it does the borders of a fractured I. The transcendental operation of the faculties is a properly paradoxical operation, opposed to their exercise under the rule of a common sense. In consequence, the harmony between the faculties can appear only in the form of a *discordant harmony*, since each communicates to the other only the violence which confronts it with its own difference and its divergence from the others. (DR 145–6)

Though the dark precursor seems to share the form of common sense in so far as it is the *condition* that enables the communication of faculties, Deleuze insists that the connection between the faculties is not the result of the imposition of an hypothesised unity of the subject or object (as is the case for common sense, which imposes the ideal of a particular mode of representation gleaned from a hypothesised form of natural and universal human reason). The 'subject' of the discordant harmony of faculties is the 'dissolved self' or 'fractured I'. Certainly Deleuze does not want to deny that the common-sense operation of the faculties results in the harmonies that produce representations. However, when the faculties attain their transcendent exercise, they are no longer constrained by the common sense but by the violence of the shock of their own powerlessness. The 'discordant harmony' of faculties operating at the transcendental level is 'paradoxical' rather than recognisable. It is paradoxical in the sense that the discordant harmony is impossible from the point of view of the empirical exercise of the faculties and necessary from the point of view of their transcendent exercise. It is in this sense of 'paradox' that Deleuze describes the dark precursor as a 'para-sense' that expresses the internal violence that forces thinking, rather than a 'common sense' that produces recognition through the imposition of an external hypothesised unity (DR 193). The dark precursor refers to the origin of experience in intensive Differences that manifest in ever changing power relations. Yet, in *Kant's Critical Philosophy* there is no sense that a common sense prior to the production of aesthetic common sense is necessary to make the faculties agree in their discordant way. There, the 'discordant accord' is spontaneous and free. Yet when 'discordant harmony' is produced in *Difference and Repetition*, Deleuze claims that the 'medium' of the communication of violence from one faculty to the next is the 'dark precursor' (DR 145). Though it seems to share the form of common sense, Deleuze insists that the connection between the faculties is not the result of the imposition of a hypothesised unity of the subject or object, as is the case for the logical and moral common senses in his reading of Kant. Yet, the aesthetic common sense is not the medium between faculties, nor does it enable communication. It is generated from the dissonance between imagination and Reason in the experience of the sublime. What is generated spontaneously from Deleuze's differential theory of faculties is a thought without Image. So why does Deleuze feel the need to introduce anything as a medium enabling communication between faculties? Perhaps this is an intentionally misleading distinction to draw attention away from the relation between aesthetic common sense and thought without Image – or perhaps even more so the connection between the 'soul' and the 'fractured I'? The most likely explanation, however, is that when Deleuze talks about the dark precursor, he is talking about the 'contemplative soul' of his earlier analyses of passive synthesis (DR 74). Joe Hughes, in his *Deleuze's Difference and Repetition*, claims that the 'contemplative soul' is equivalent to the spontaneous imagination. From this perspective, one might say that the dark precursor is the passage from one faculty to another as the drama of the unfolding of powerlessness within power playing itself out. Deleuze gives to this drama the name 'problematic Ideas'.

Problematic Ideas

Problematic Ideas are a crucial but difficult notion in Deleuze's work – they feature prominently in his theory of faculties, his epistemology, as well as his intensive ontology. It would be impossible to explain all the complexity of problematic Ideas here, so the focus will be on clarifying their relation to the differential theory of faculties and the account of the genesis of a thought without Image. To understand problematic Ideas in these contexts, it is sufficient to understand their apparently paradoxical place as both the transcendental ground of thinking and the products of thought. They are distinct from Deleuze's notion of 'encounters', and from Kant's notion of 'problematic Ideas'.

Unlike with Kant, for Deleuze the faculty of Reason is not the sole generator of problematic Ideas. They are produced by all the faculties and in fact 'furnish the conditions under which the faculties attain their superior exercise' (DR 146). They are not, however, equivalent with encounters. Though on the surface problematic Ideas seem to perform the same function as encounters – in so far as the latter also supply the conditions for the superior exercise of the faculties – problematic Ideas do not have their origin in sensibility. The question of the origin of problematic Ideas is tricky for Deleuze. Though he claims that they concern all the faculties, they nonetheless 'have a very special relationship to pure thought' (DR 194). As Deleuze explains it, thought attains its transcendent exercise at the extremity of the 'fuse of violence which, from one Idea to another, first sets in motion sensibility and its *sentiendum*', and Ideas are born of this extremity (DR 194). Indeed, thought must be understood in its highest form as the expression or actualisation of problematic Ideas. The difficulty with this initial formulation of their origin, however, is that it makes it appear as if problematic Ideas are required for the generation of problematic Ideas. If problematic Ideas are what set sensibility in motion but are also the products of that motion, then they seem to be self-generated. However, this problem disappears and the real problem emerges when we see that Deleuze associates the notion of 'problematic Ideas' with a knot of other concepts, including

'Ideas', 'problems' and 'questions'. Though Deleuze often uses these terms interchangeably, there are important distinctions to be made. 'Problems' designate an open yet 'unitary and systematic' symbolic 'field' that orients experiences so that answers 'form precisely cases of solution' (DR 168). 'Questions' are what force faculties into their transcendent exercise. 'Ideas' are generated at the extremity of the violence that questions pose to the faculties – that is, Ideas are the products of thought at the end of a chain reaction involving all of the faculties. These Ideas, in turn, form new problematic fields for which new questions must be generated and new Ideas formed.

Deleuze's alternative to the dogmatic Image of thought presents problems as the transcendental ground of thinking, questions as the genetic elements of thought, and Ideas as the products of thought. This explanation has the advantage of reconciling the passages from *Difference and Repetition* that suggest problematic Ideas are generated from encounters with other passages that suggest that encounters are generated by problematic Ideas. Both can be the case when problems, questions and Ideas are distinguished. The apparently paradoxical place of problematic Ideas as both the transcendental ground of thinking and the products of thought can be explained by these distinctions as well.

The encounter is a violence constituted by pure Difference, and this Difference takes the form of a problem. At the extremity of the violence of the encounter both thinking and the Idea are constituted. Ideas problematise each faculty and even themselves in such a way as to open whatever they touch for the mark of its difference. Like questions that beget more questions (or Ideas in their wild and untamed state, sparking new Ideas), thinking is encountering Difference but in a constant confrontation and exchange which forces thought to 'think otherwise'. It is thus that the ontological becomes inseparable from the moral and the practical. Deleuze is clear when, late in *Difference and Repetition*, he says of the 'distortion' of thought brought about by the dogmatic Image that, 'if the truth be told, none of this would amount to much were it not for the moral presuppositions and practical implications of such a distortion' (DR 268). Those moral presuppositions can only be contested in a real way by focusing on the preparatory education for encounters that Deleuze sets up with his work on the passivity/limitation of the faculties (and later with the passive syntheses). The notion of problematic Ideas as the vehicle for the reinvestment of critical practice into the passive flows establishes the fundamental starting point for an ethics based on habit-formation in critical thinking. Thus, critique, in the specific Deleuzian sense of an evaluation of the limits and powers of the faculties, has an important role in the creation of a thought without Image, in the process of deterritorialisation, and in the resistance to fascism that Foucault saw as the fundamental ethical standpoint articulated by Deleuze and Guattari in *Anti-Oedipus*.

Notes

1. See especially Robert Bernasconi, 'Will the Real Kant Please Stand Up', *Radical Philosophy* 117 (2003), pp. 13–22.
2. Hughes, *Philosophy After Deleuze*, pp. 14–19. As Hughes writes: 'The only way to get to the heart of Deleuze's project was to give up the search of key lines and disconnected passages and try instead to designate the underlying, monotonous structure. This structure characterises a genesis or a process of self-transcendence, and this means among many things that each moment has to be understood in its functional relations to other moments of the structure . . . this structure is monotonous – that is to say, because it repeats itself in each of Deleuze's major texts – there is a proliferation of terms for each moment' (p. 36).
3. Diane Beddoes, 'Deleuze, Kant, and Indifference', in *Deleuze and Philosophy: The Difference Engineer*, p. 28.
4. Ibid. pp. 29, 30.
5. Ibid. p. 31.
6. 'For nothing can be said in advance, one cannot prejudge the outcome of research: it may be that some well-known faculties – too well known – turn out to have no proper limit, no verbal adjective, because they are imposed and have an exercise only under the form of common sense. It may turn out, on the other hand, that new faculties arise, faculties which were repressed by that form of common sense. For a doctrine in general, there is nothing regrettable in this uncertainty about the outcome of research, this complexity in the study of the particular case of each faculty: on the contrary, transcendental empiricism is the only way to avoid tracing the transcendental from the outlines of the empirical' (DR 143–4).
7. As Ian Buchanan has persuasively argued: 'the assemblage is not a thing and it does not consist of things. I would even go so far as to say the assemblage does not have any content, it is a purely formal arrangement or ordering that functions as a mechanism of inclusion and exclusion' ('Assemblage Theory, or, The Future of an Illusion', *Deleuze Studies* 11:3 (2017), p. 465). This article includes Buchanan's helpful analysis of the meaning and illusory 'plain language' sense of 'assemblage' used in the social sciences (458).
8. 'For as reason is not competent to guide the will with certainty in regard

to its objects and the satisfaction of all our wants (which it to some extent even multiplies), this being an end to which an implanted instinct would have led with much greater certainty; and since, nevertheless, reason is imparted to us as a practical faculty, i.e., as one which is to have influence on the will, therefore, admitting that nature generally in the distribution of her capacities has adapted the means to the end, its true destination must be to produce a will, not merely good as a means to something else, but good in itself, for which reason was absolutely necessary. This will then, though not indeed the sole and complete good, must be the supreme good and the condition of every other, even of the desire of happiness.' Immanuel Kant, *Groundwork of the Metaphysics of Morals*, trans. Mary Gregor, Cambridge: Cambridge University Press, 1997, pp. 9–10.

9. For Kant, there are two types of representations: intuitions and concepts. These two map onto two types of faculties: sensibility and understanding, respectively. While both have an impure, empirical aspect, they both contain a purely formal one as well. For sensibility, the formal aspects are the a priori forms of intuition in space and time. They are the condition of the possibility of any intuition. The formal aspects of the understanding, on the other hand, are the a priori forms of concepts in the categories, or, the different ways that the unity of concepts can be thought. Though Deleuze does not mention this characterisation of the faculties' pure and impure forms, it neatly fits with his characterisation of the faculties' higher and lower forms.

10. Daniel Smith, 'Deleuze, Kant, and the Theory of Immanent Ideas', in *Deleuze and Philosophy*, ed. Constantin Boundas, Edinburgh: Edinburgh University Press, 2006, p. 51.

11. While Deleuze does not seem to believe that all forms of violence are the same, his relationship to violence is a legitimate question being asked by scholars. See especially Ann Murphy, 'The Remainder: Between Symbolic and Material Violence', in *Philosophy and the Return of Violence*, ed. C. Yates and N. Eckstrand, New York: Continuum, 2011, pp. 189–201.

12. New York's Museum of Modern Art, at http://www.moma.org/collection/object.php?object_id=80103 (last accessed 27 September 2017).

13. What is encountered is not blue as such – it is the problem that is solved by the blueness. Intensity in the encounter is something subjects typically ignore but with which their bodies are always dealing.

14. See Jerold Abrams, 'Cinema and the Aesthetics of the Dynamical Sublime: Kant, Deleuze, and Heidegger on the Architecture of Film', *Film and Philosophy* 7 (2003), pp. 60–76. Abrams is primarily interested in the relation between the sublime and film, which he sees connected in Deleuze's cinema books. He tries to mediate between two interpretations of what Deleuze means when he makes this connection.

The Theory of Faculties

He assumes a Kantian point of view toward film by focusing on the experience of the voyeur fragmented by time and on Hitchcock's films. He believes film is, at its best, a pursuit of the experience of the dynamical sublime.

15. Deleuze foregrounds the distinction between differences in kind and in degree in his 1966 work *Bergsonism*, trans. Hugh Tomlinson and Barbara Habberjam, New York: Zone Books, 1991.
16. For an excellent comparison of Deleuze and Foucault on the concept of the limit, see James Brusseau, *Isolated Experiences: Gilles Deleuze and the Solitudes of Reversed Platonism*, Albany: SUNY Press, 1998. Brusseau characterises Deleuze's 'understated' conception of limitation as 'how production determines and defines itself' (p. 45). Similarly, he characterises Foucault's use of the concept in terms of a vocabulary shift: rather than thinking of limitation in terms of opposition, he thinks of it in terms of 'sovereign production. Rather than negation, limitation is conceived by Foucault as affirmation' (p. 46). This sort of limitation acts according to rules, but self-imposed ones, produced as a boundary that is generated from the action itself.
17. 'There is a crucial experience of difference and a corresponding experiment: every time we find ourselves confronted or bound by a limitation or an opposition, we should ask what such a situation presupposes. It presupposes a swarm of differences, a pluralism of free, wild or untamed differences; a properly differential and original space and time; all of which persist alongside the simplifications of limitation and opposition' (DR 50).
18. Intrinsic is distinguished from internal in so far as Deleuze claims that 'intrinsic' applies to the essence (DR 51).
19. Kant uses the German *seelenerhebende*, which literally translates as 'soul-elevating' (CJ §29 'General remark on the exposition of aesthetic reflective judgements').
20. CJ 'Introduction: III On the critique of the power of judgement, as a means for combining the two parts of philosophy into one whole', and CJ 'Introduction: IX On the connection of the legislations of understanding and reason through the power of judgment'.

3
Immanent Critique

Transcendental Immanence

In *Difference and Repetition* Deleuze openly admires Kant's critique for revealing the transcendental realm (DR 135), for bringing Time into the conditions of experience, for inaugurating the idea of the passive self (DR 86), for substituting of the idea of internal illusions for the concept of error (DR 136), for its simultaneously destructive and creative capacity (DR 132, 139), and for that brief moment in the *Critique of Judgement* when it reveals sublimity as engendering aesthetic common sense and thereby rises above its simple standpoint of conditioning to achieve that of genesis. But while Deleuze argues that Kant seemed poised to sweep away the dogmatic Image of thought, he also strongly argued that the Kantian critique ultimately fails, for several reasons: It elevates simple empirical examples to transcendental models (the problem of 'psychologism') (DR 135); it does not ultimately overcome the dualism of concept and intuition; it retreats from the standpoint of genesis in favour of conditioning; and it understands problems in terms of their solvability (the problem of 'extrinsicism'). Yet all of these reasons can be traced back to one fatal flaw: Kant's failure to push his thought beyond its common sense subjective biases and conformism. This flaw is what Deleuze calls Kant's 'moralism' (DR 4, 132, 197), and it is so significant that the dogmatic Image of thought is synonymously referred to throughout *Difference and Repetition* as the 'moral Image' of thought (DR 131). Deleuze contests the dogmatic Image of thought in the way that he claims Kant could not: by subjecting it to a 'radical critique' (DR 132).

According to this radical critique, the Kantian critical model Deleuze has laid out must undergo its own critique and submit to a series of radical modifications aimed at the 'common sense' presuppositions of morality that Deleuze believes Kant failed to abandon. So, even though Deleuze laments Kant's failure to take his critique far enough, he does not consider this an inherent failure of the critical

Immanent Critique

project itself. Rather than abandon that project, Deleuze attempts to renew it. His radical critique thus begins not by overthrowing the original Kantian initiative (the effort to turn the examination of the relationships and limits of power inward) but by applying that initiative to a systematic evaluation of the dogmatic Image of thought and the moral presuppositions on which it is built (DR 132).[1] Deleuze writes that a philosophy without presuppositions:

> would take as its point of departure a radical critique of the [dogmatic] image and the 'postulates' it implies. It would find its difference or its true beginning, not in an agreement with the *pre-philosophical* Image but in a rigorous struggle against this image, which it would denounce as *non-philosophical*. (DR 132)

Only through producing the radical critique, which must be a 'rigorous struggle against' the dogmatic Image, will Deleuze be in a position to offer the new, differential, theory of faculties and a thought 'freed' from any Image (DR 132). By destroying the dogmatic Image of thought, thought is liberated from the presuppositions that chain it to repetitions of the same: what is already recognised, recognisable, known and knowable. This is the primary goal of *Difference and Repetition*: to discover a way of thinking that does not merely reproduce the old forms of thinking under new names, and that resists stagnating into simply another form of common-sense thinking. In other words, to break with *doxa*.

Deleuze's destruction and radicalisation of critique can be understood through four figures: its level of analysis, its object, its practice and its internal logic. These respond to the four failures Deleuze sees in Kant: transcendence, psychologism, conditioning and extrinsicism. It is possible to discern the trajectory of Deleuze's philosophy through these figures as they echo and mutate from his early through to his later works.

Level of analysis

In the first pages of *Kant's Critical Philosophy*, Deleuze shows how Kant's definition of philosophy reveals a 'struggle ... against empiricism and against dogmatic rationalism' (KCP 1). While it may seem that empiricism and dogmatic rationalism have little in common, on Deleuze's reading both are predicated on the assumption that reason's ends are not determined by reason itself but externally, and that therefore they both require the additional assumption of a pre-established harmony to account for the relation of subject and object. In *Kant's Critical Philosophy*, the important features of the problem are the assumption of the externality of Reason's ends and of a pre-established harmony to overcome that externality. Compare this to the first pages of the third chapter of *Difference and Repetition*, which begin with a meditation on the problem of beginning in philosophy. The problem, as Deleuze sees it, is that 'beginning means eliminating all presuppositions', but the history of philosophy is dogged by a subjective presupposition that links thinking itself with simple recognition (DR 129). The problem with using recognition as the model for all thought is that recognition requires the presupposition of a 'common sense' as the condition of the harmony of faculties necessary for recognition to take place. This 'common sense' is external to thought but nonetheless pre-establishes what can count as thought. The important features of the problem are again the externality of 'common sense' to thought and its necessary assumption for pre-establishing both thought's equivalence with recognition and the harmony between faculties that recognition represents. What becomes clear from these descriptions is that the Kant of *Kant's Critical Philosophy* and the Deleuze of *Difference and Repetition* are both troubled by explanations of our faculties that assume something external to the faculties and are then forced to assume a pre-established harmony to make the assumption of externality work. In other words, both begin their philosophical inquiries by problematising transcendence. Both, then, situate their work's analysis at the transcendental level. However, since Kant's transcendental critique ultimately does not overcome the dualism of concept and intuition, Deleuze resituates the critique in terms of its immanence. What Deleuze gains by describing Kant's difference from empiricism and dogmatic rationalism in terms of an opposing account of the source of reason's ends is a catalyst to foreground the significance of the ideal of immanence in the critical approach.

It is sometimes argued that Deleuze's Kantianism ends by the time of the *Capitalism and Schizophrenia* project with Guattari. The suggestion is that Deleuze abandons the transcendental approach characteristic of his earlier works in favour of a thoroughgoing materialism. Eugene Holland, for instance, argues that schizoanalysis draws principally 'on the three great materialists of the last century – Freud, Marx, and Nietzsche'.[2] Holland is correct to focus on the importance of these three figures for the materialist psychiatry developed by Deleuze and Guattari, however, it would not be amiss

Immanent Critique

to add to his interpretation the crucial Kantian dimension of the schizoanalytic approach. Not only do Deleuze and Guattari attach the project of schizoanalysis to a version of Kantian critique, the goal of schizoanalysis is an evaluation of the limits and powers (schizes and desiring-production) of faculties (machines) so as to establish the illegitimate (transcendent) and legitimate (immanent) 'uses' or 'exercises' of the syntheses constitutive of the unconscious (AO 74–5). As Deleuze and Guattari state in *Anti-Oedipus*:

> In what he termed the critical revolution, Kant intended to discover criteria immanent to understanding so as to distinguish the legitimate and illegitimate use of the syntheses of consciousness. In the name of *transcendental* philosophy (immanence of criteria), he therefore denounced the transcendent use of syntheses such as appeared in metaphysics. In like fashion we are compelled to say that psychoanalysis has its metaphysics – its name is Oedipus. And that a revolution – this time materialist – can proceed only by way of a critique of Oedipus, by denouncing the illegitimate use of the syntheses of the unconscious as found in Oedipal psychoanalysis, so as to rediscover a transcendental unconscious defined by the immanence of its criteria, and a corresponding practice that we shall call schizoanalysis. (AO 75)

For Holland, Deleuze and Guattari make this connection to Kant in order 'to illustrate by analogy their own procedure'.[3] But as the above passage illustrates, the connection between the Kantian critique and schizoanalysis is more than just analogical. At the level of the analysis the approaches are identical: identifying the transcendent use of the faculties' syntheses and replacing them with immanent/transcendental uses. In *A Thousand Plateaus* Deleuze and Guattari develop the concept of the nomadological war machine as a model for minoritarian political and social assemblages that operates as a critical consciousness, constantly questioning and contesting social norms and presuppositions (TP 417). Though the language changes dramatically – and in some cases justifiably – toward a more materialist perspective, the underlying commitments remain largely unchanged.

Object

In *Kant's Critical Philosophy* Deleuze introduces the idea of 'immanent critique' as the 'so-called transcendental method' that seeks to determine 'the true nature of reason's interests or ends' and 'the means of realising these interests' (KCP 3). Kant's critique can be distinguished from other forms of critique (such as Descartes' or Hume's sceptical versions) in so far as it is not fundamentally negative. Rather, Kantian critique examines the structure and limitations of the faculty of Reason so as to properly distinguish and synthesise conflicting perspectives at the deeper level marked out by that examination: the level of the transcendental. Traditionally, Kant's transcendental is understood as the level of conditions of experience. Deleuze initially follows this tradition, but emphasises the importance of a theory of faculties for any examination of the transcendental. As is well known, Kant's contribution to the debate over how to justify subjective beliefs about objective states – what has come to be known as his 'transcendental turn' – was to rephrase this problem in terms of subjects' capacities of experiencing. For Kant, what subjects experience is determined by what they *can* experience, that is, by their capacities, powers or faculties. Faculties are thus not actual experience, but the conditions of experience. As such, they straddle the line between transcendent objects and subjects' inner experience of those objects. This line between – the transcendental – is the level that Kant believes makes the relation between transcendent objects and subjects' inner experience of them possible. In this way he transforms the problem of the relationship between subjects and objects into a problem of the relation between faculties. Faculties are thus the content of the transcendental domain and the proper objects of critical examination. The critical practices running as a theme throughout the Deleuzian philosophical story all have in common this starting point in transcendental immanence and the object of the faculties, whether these be described as habits, drives, forces, relations, desires or machines.

The move characteristic of immanent critique is that the level of faculties is attained by 'internalising' problems. When confronted with a problem, such as that of subject/object dualism, immanent critique seeks the internal forces that gave rise to the problem. Those internal forces refer to the faculties as capacities for experience rather than experience itself. After identifying the faculties, immanent critique must explain them in terms that are internal to the faculties themselves. Thus the faculties are described in terms of their intrinsic power, which can be determined by identifying each faculty's limits. Christian Kerslake anticipated this reading in his dense and insightful 2004 article 'Deleuze, Kant, and the Question of Metacritique' when he wrote that 'we are now to understand the goal of critique as the full realisation of reason's power to problematise. The critique of the "natural" state of reason, which involves the isolation of the difference in kind of reason from the other faculties, will thus facilitate the realisation of reason.'[4] A truly immanent critique condemns not only faculties' attempts to exceed their limits but also their failure to reach their limits. This reveals another characteristic of immanent critique: its goal of determining the means of realising the faculties' superior exercise at the limit of what they can do. But it also reveals one of the practical aspects hidden within this story.

Because the moral interests smuggled into critique are conceived by Deleuze as subjective presuppositions, there is no way of knowing whether Kant was aware of them. This is an important point to make in order to resist the interpretation that Deleuze's reading of Kant is itself guilty of psychologism. Deleuze is not merely charging Kant with psychological predilections or desires that influenced the way he practised critique. Rather, he is diagnosing a problem that he sees as endemic to a particular way of doing philosophy that dogmatically begins by assuming all thought is recognition. Kant represents a way of thinking that operates at the limits of the dogmatic approach to philosophy but ultimately does not go far enough. What would be far enough, from Deleuze's perspective, is for immanent critical evaluation to start not from predetermined 'ends' at all, but from an examination of the real powers and limits of the faculties. Deleuze's insistence on treating the faculties primarily in terms of the expression of their power rather than in terms of 'ends' separate from that expression can be understood as an attempt to circumvent the subjective presuppositions Kant introduced into his Critiques and allow the faculties to speak for themselves. In this way Deleuze attempts to break with *doxa* by first attending to an analysis of the faculties on their own terms. After all, 'the point of view of an ethics is: of what are you capable, what can you do? Hence a return to this sort of cry of Spinoza's: what can a body do? We never know in advance what a body can do. We never know how we're organised and how the modes of existence are enveloped in somebody.'[5] This represents a clear parallel between Deleuze's work in *Difference and Repetition* and his and Guattari's work in *Capitalism and Schizophrenia*. Moreover, as Joe Hughes and others have noted, 'desiring-machine' is 'simply an alternate expression for the transcendental unconscious', which is a process of production comprising three distinct, passive, moments: a connective synthesis, a disjunctive synthesis and a conjunctive synthesis.[6] Whereas the desiring-machine parallels the trajectory of the faculties in their function as syntheses, the notion of 'partial objects', a concept which expresses the standpoint of materialism with greater force, parallels the trajectory of faculties in their first sense (from *Kant's Critical Philosophy*) as the basic units synthesised (TP 36). In both cases, the objects of the critique remain the same throughout the oeuvre.

Practice

'Extrinsicism' is the problem, first identified by Salomon Maïmon, of positing the faculties of sensibility and understanding as different in kind, and thus still subject to a substance dualism that only a pre-established harmony or constant divine intervention could overcome (DR 180). Kant's goal had been to overcome the dualism of subject and object by repositioning the debate at the level of the conditions of experience understood in terms of faculties. However, the subject/object dualism was not overcome in this move, merely pushed back to the level of the relation between the 'passive' faculty of sensibility and the 'active' faculties of understanding, Reason and imagination. Deleuze argues that Kant dealt with this problem in two ways: first by developing an account of a synthesis carried out by the imagination that applies the understanding's form of unity to sensations (thus mediating between the passive and active faculties), then by hypothesising the 'common sense' as a necessary condition for explaining the harmony between all the faculties (DR 173, CPR A326/B383–4, CPR A669/B697). In Deleuze's eyes, both solutions failed: the first because it leaves unanswered the question of how the imagination can carry out a conceptual determination (imagination and understanding being different in kind as well), and the second because the idea of 'common sense' reintroduces the very pre-established harmony Kant meant to avoid.

Kant recognised that he had not truly solved the problem of extrinsicism and in the *Critique of Judgement* attempted once again to overcome it by going beyond his account of conditions to a deeper account of the genesis of aesthetic common sense from the way the sub-representative (indeed, unrepresentable) sensation of sublimity reveals and draws out the powers immanent within the faculties.[7] Only a genetic account of the emergence of harmony between the faculties can overcome the problem of extrinsicism because an account based on conditions could never offer anything more than the hypothesis of a substrate of unity, which smuggles in pre-established harmony and all of the implicit biases associated with it. As such, genesis, unlike

Immanent Critique

conditioning, can reveal the emergence of the dogmatic Image of thought rather than simply assuming it. It is because of the power of this genetic analysis, which Deleuze sees as the apotheosis of critique, that Deleuze's transcendental empiricism relies on it for his model of a differential theory of faculties.

There are several points to emphasise about this story. First, Deleuze claims that in this account, at last, the accord of faculties is not simply assumed as a condition but is produced in a genesis. The accord of faculties is produced in the dissention between imagination and Reason. The feeling of expansion in the soul produced by this dissention then unifies the faculties, creating the aesthetic common sense. In the previous accounts of common sense, critique remained at the level of conditions of representations when it simply assumed a priori certain hierarchies of relations between faculties (i.e. certain forms of common sense) as necessary for the very possibility of those representations. Genetic critique, by contrast, grounds in the singular experience of the sublime a *felt* unity of the subject applying not to assumptions but to the powers immanent within faculties themselves.

There is thus also a parallel here between *Kant's Critical Philosophy* and *Difference and Repetition*'s critical practice: seeking the genesis of experience rather than the conditions of experience. Much of Deleuze's reading of the failure of Kant's critical project revolves around what Deleuze calls 'conditioning' critique rather than 'genetic' critique. While Deleuze claims that Kant made the immanent internalising move of shifting the problem of the relation of subject and object to that of the relation of the subjective faculties of sensibility and understanding, the question of how passive sensibility and active understanding achieve an accord nevertheless remained, since the faculties of sensibility and understanding (like all the faculties for Kant) differ in nature. According to Deleuze, Kant's attempt to introduce 'common sense' as an inherent 'good nature of the faculties' to explain their accord implicitly transposed the very assumption of pre-established harmony his immanent critique was supposed to reject (KCP 22). On Deleuze's reading, however, Kant realised this difficulty and understood that unless he could provide a genetic account of common sense as the principle of the accord of faculties the immanence of the critical perspective would be lost and his entire critical philosophy would fall (KCP 23). Thus was born Kant's account of the genesis of aesthetic common sense from the experience of sublimity in the *Critique of Judgement*. It is this account that Deleuze uses as the model for how thought realises its superior exercise by producing a thought without Image, and this model that he considers Kant to have betrayed in the teleological, hierarchical story about the moral priority of the end of Reason.

Though this reading is meant to develop a trajectory (rather than a break) from the transcendental approach to the materialist approach, it is important to note that the vocabulary of 'transcendental immanence' used here diverges from Deleuze's preferred vocabulary of 'transcendental empiricism', which, it might be argued, would more clearly demonstrate this trajectory. The simple way of describing Deleuze's transcendental empiricism is to say that it seeks the genesis of real experience rather than the conditions of possible experience. Its goal is an analysis of the *internal* differences at the root of the genesis of experience. But, as has already been shown, experience in this sense does not refer to everyday experiences already subjected to the form of common sense. Deleuze reasons that his transcendentalism counts as a form of empiricism because he cannot anticipate what the internal differences will be and so must look for them in real, actual (but not everyday) experience. The important distinction is that rather than looking for internal differences in possible experience, the transcendental empiricist must look for them in real experience. Real experience is concrete and present, as opposed to an abstract and futural possibility. The difference between the real and the possible is like the difference between a pair of trousers tailored to someone's specific measurements and a one-size-fits-all pair of trousers. The tailored trousers fit a real person, whereas the one-size-fits-all trousers meant to fit every possible person likely actually fit no one. Real experience is preferable to possible experience because it fits the actual situation. The difference between genesis and conditioning, on the other hand, is that while genesis describes the emergence of a phenomenon, conditions hypothesise facts without which the phenomenon would not exist. So, a genetic account of Bertrand Russell, for instance, would detail Russell's development from the perspective of the powers and problems internal to his growth, whereas a conditioning account would simply identify the fact (external to Russell himself) that he had to have parents in order to exist at all. While the conditioning account identifies facts external to the phenomenon at issue, the genetic account offers an internal determination of what makes a phenomenon what it is. The focus on the internal powers and limitations of faculties undertaken here justifies the use of the term 'immanence' rather than 'empiricism', which in the *Capitalism and Schizophrenia* project is arguably the preferred term.

Immanent Critique

INTERNAL LOGIC

Finally, there is also a parallel between *Kant's Critical Philosophy* and *Difference and Repetition*'s critiques at the level of their internal logics. In the *Critique of Pure Reason* critique is evaluative, limiting and even destructive. Yet these apparently negative activities make something positive possible (CPR Bxxiv–xxv). For Kant, critique's limiting of speculative reason frees one to pursue 'an absolutely necessary practical use of pure reason': realising moral good in the world (CPR Bxxv). Critique's limitations and evaluations are in the service of realising the interests of the faculty of Reason. What this means is that critical evaluation, limitation and destruction are positive and creative. While there is much about this story that Deleuze resists, what he seeks to recuperate in his reading of Kant's critical project is the complex logic by which a form of violence produces powerlessness that becomes power through a process of internalisation. This logic is visible operating at the very inception of Kant's project. His description of the development of the critical perspective is a perfect example. It begins with a description of the problem that 'awoke' him from his 'dogmatic slumber': Hume's sceptical attack on causal reasoning forced Kant to acknowledge how difficult it is to justify knowledge claims. All prior attempts to ground the relationship between the subject and object had proved unsatisfactory. Kant's frustration and avowed sense of powerlessness in the face of Hume's criticism led him to reverse the terms of the discussion. Instead of supposing that our knowledge must conform to objects, Kant suggests considering how objects might conform to our knowledge instead (CPR Bxvi). Knowledge thus comes to depend on the capacities or faculties of the knower rather than on the object itself. The logic here is that the problem (Hume's criticism) imposes itself violently, forcing Kant to acknowledge his limitations – yet it is these same limitations that open a new path: knowers are limited by what they *can* know, so if the focus shifts to those limitations (i.e. the faculties of knowing themselves), they can be moved 'beyond' to build a foundation for knowledge in general. The 'beyond' Kant subsequently discovers takes the form of his much-contested 'synthetic a prioris'.

This same logic is repeated in Kant's account of the genesis of aesthetic common sense from the experience of sublimity in the *Critique of Judgement*. The experience of the sublime forces humans to measure themselves against the apparent omnipotence of Nature. It forces humans to accept their own limitation and insufficiency, but at the same time allows them to discover in their own limited and insufficient faculty of Reason a presentation of the 'infinite', of their own souls as foundations of the aesthetic common sense and of their own superiority over Nature. According to the logic described above, the sublime is the violent shock that awakens the faculty of imagination to its powerlessness – stretching it 'to the extremity of its power' (KCP 50) – but that powerlessness is internalised when it represents 'to itself the inaccessibility of the rational Idea' represented in the sublime and makes this inaccessibility 'something which is present in sensible nature' (KCP 51). Human imagination thus 'exceeds' its own limits by grasping what is at the very limit of its power. As we saw in Chapter 2, this logic reappears again in Deleuze's differential theory of faculties in *Difference and Repetition*. There, the violence of the encounter plunges each faculty in its turn into an involuntary adventure in which the faculty 'is born to the extreme point of its dissolution' where it confronts what is, for it, ungraspable from the point of view of its empirical exercise. However, that limitation leads the faculty to its transcendent exercise where it grasps what that faculty alone can grasp. Each faculty thus discovers its unique power as its limit or powerlessness at the level of its empirical exercise.

The relationship Deleuze has to Kant can be summarised as follows: Deleuze sees in Kant's critical perspective something deeply illuminating, but Kant betrayed that perspective, forcing Deleuze to work against him in the interest of rescuing what Deleuze considers still valuable. That is why we get a kind of double reading of Kant in Deleuze's use/abuse of him that is so deeply conflicted. This logic recurs in Deleuze's simultaneous use of the dynamic between activity and passivity suggested by Kant's introduction of the empty form of Time into the I with his attempt to criticise and distance his theory from what he perceives as a betrayal of that dynamic in Kant's hard distinction between passive and active faculties. The movement from powerlessness to power through an immanent approach is the archetype for every Deleuzian story, operating beneath even the account of production in the later 'materialist' version.

Dramatising Vulnerability

As we have seen, Deleuzian critique is the practice of evaluating the immanent limits and powers of the faculties through an analysis of their genesis from intensive differences. But the account as it has unfolded so far has set aside a crucial detail about Deleuze's differential theory of the faculties. This is Deleuze's insistence that the experience of the encounter that sparks the fuse of thought is affective, not cognitive. If this is the case, it is fair to ask in what sense a critical practice, undertaken actively and intentionally, could generate the fundamental disequilibrium necessary for new thought to arise. This is a question that has a long history in French poststructuralist stories. For someone like Foucault, if it is impossible to get outside of one's historical epoch and its conditions of truth and knowledge, how can the perspective from within ever effectively render strange the experience of being within? Would not the experience of strangeness need to come from without? Deleuze at least is clear that the rupture of the normal in experience comes from the encounter, which draws its power directly from Difference itself, which is not outside since there is no 'outside' for this thoroughly immanent philosophy. But even if that is the case, the relationship between the encounter, thought, newness and critique remains undetermined.

In *The Invention of a People*, Janae Sholtz develops Deleuze's notion of the encounter in relation to art's revolutionary potential to create new forms of community. She reads Deleuze's conception of art as that which opens 'a window onto the vital flux of immanent life', 'invokes the radical, inhuman forces of becoming', and acts as 'a catalyst for becoming minor, for the transformation of politics'.[8] Art is privileged as the medium of the Event – that which transports the sublime force of the encounter that exceeds representation, igniting the drama that forces thinking, opening the human to self-overcoming, and providing the vertiginous space for political resistance. Sholtz explores the work of artists such as Kafka, Bacon, Klee, Rimbaud and Jarry – to name just a few – as exemplars of art's power to disrupt, contest and inspire. As she writes, 'encounters with art offer a paradigm of aesthetic living, engaging with and creating affects that literally transform one's world and being'.[9] On Sholtz's reading there is an ontological as well as an ethical exigency to the experience of art. Through the openness to art, subjects become nomadic. In one of the most beautiful passages of her book, Sholtz describes Dick Higgins' *A Thousand Symphonies*, in which orchestral paper was riddled with bullet holes and music composed from the resulting scars: '*A Thousand Symphonies* catalyses the political and social arena, as an example of the transmutation of violence and the material triggers of violence into an affective *logos* about violence.'[10] Higgins' art inspires philosophical thinking on violence, developing a new sensibility to the outside, that is, to what had been unthought.

Here and throughout her work Sholtz's background postulation is that she is addressing other philosophers. Despite the broader political implications she is drawing, her analysis intervenes primarily for people who are already 'cultured'. In the pages on Higgins' *A Thousand Symphonies*, she is developing an example of art preparing a critical consciousness. However, it is fair to ask (and Sholtz anticipates this line of questioning) what preparation had to go on before art's power could take hold. Perhaps there is an opening here that would allow us to augment Sholtz's reading with an account of the development of sensitivity to art. Perhaps, rather than seeing a unidirectional movement from affective to critical consciousness, the movement between the affective and the critical is more like a spiral. Moreover, perhaps an attitude cultivated – even habituated – through critique is the preparatory attunement necessary for experiencing the sublimity of the encounter with art.

In *The Critique of Judgement* Kant writes 'without the development of moral ideas, that which we, prepared by culture, call sublime will appear merely repellent to the unrefined person' (§29 CJ). This is an issue that haunts philosophical theories that tie moral development to the experience of art. They merely push back the question of transformation. The real question is: How does art become appreciable as a rift? How does one begin to experience art as an encounter rather than simply as repulsive (as many perceive Bacon), irrelevant (as Jarry's work might be seen) or abstruse (as Klee's might be)? Sholtz's answer in *The Invention of a People* oscillates between two poles. At the one pole she justifiably emphasises that the affective dimension of human nature is, for Deleuze, primitive. It is the most basic medium through which bodies interact with the world. So there can be no prior attunement that does not arise in affect. At the other pole she acknowledges that 'we must be able to experience our distress rather than cover it over'.[11] This is a capability that exceeds the bare experience of art. After all, the affective, or sensibility itself, can be over-determined and limited by homogenising and stabilising categories. Thought is not the only faculty at risk from this sedative occupation. It is a problem, ultimately, of pedagogy. In Deleuze's terminology, it is a problem of culture or *paideia*. Sholtz anticipates but does develop this point when, in the context of a discussion of Rimbaud, she writes: 'Thought is not its own author. We do not construct or control, but what we can do is cultivate vulnerability with respect to sheer immanence and affectivity. Without the development of this raw sensibility we may remain unequal to the event.'[12] This idea of cultivating vulnerability to become worthy of the event is the precise point that it is crucial to build upon. Indeed, if the ethical exigency of the way of life implicated by Sholtz's reading of the relationship between community, earth and aesthetics is taken seriously, then a critical pedagogy whose aim is the cultivation of an ethos of openness, of questioning, of welcoming the undoing of our security in our knowledge, even unto the undoing of ourselves, is necessary. This is a task for thinking about thinking about art – one that can and should awaken our sensitivity to encounters through art.

Again it is Kant who provides Deleuze with the model for how to awaken sensitivity to encounters in the way Sholtz requires. For Kant as well as for Deleuze, in order for the faculties to transcend their limits up to the point of generating a thought without Image, a particular form of cultivation is required. This form of cultivation is determined by the Greek notion of *paideia* understood as a 'violent training' in evaluating presuppositions (DR 165). In *Kant's Critical Philosophy*, after describing how the sense of the sublime prepares humans for the moral law, Deleuze's next sentence is: 'This is why the common sense which corresponds to the feeling of the sublime is inseparable from a "culture" as the movement of its genesis (CJ §29)' (KCP 51–2). For German thinkers in the late eighteenth century, the word 'culture'[13] was closely associated with its roots in the idea of cultivation – particularly the cultivation of soil. The question of agriculture is how to get the most out of seeds, and the methods of cultivation increase seed productivity. In an extension of this idea, the question of 'culture' for Kant and his contemporaries was how to get the most out of humans by developing the mind through education and training. Philosophy and what we now call the humanities were believed to be the primary avenue for the sort of education necessary for cultivating human minds.

If the context of Kant's writing is an understanding of culture as preparatory education, the question of what he believed humans are being prepared for remains.[14] In §29 of the *Critique of Judgement* Kant suggests that culture prepares humans for the experience of the sublime:

> There are innumerable things in beautiful nature concerning which we immediately require consensus with our own judgement from everyone else and can also, without being especially prone to error, expect it; but we cannot promise ourselves that our judgement concerning the sublime in nature will so readily find acceptance by others. For a far greater culture, not merely of the aesthetic power of judgement, but also of the

cognitive faculties on which that is based, seems to be requisite in order to be able to make a judgement about this excellence of the objects of nature.

The interpretation of this passage has been a point of contention in Kantian scholarship. The question is whether Kant considered the cultivation of taste as the propaedeutic for morality or morality as the basis for taste. Deleuze's solution is to understand cultivation as the development of moral feeling, which is simply the first step in the development of morality itself. So, when Kant writes that, 'without the development of moral ideas, that which we, prepared by culture, call sublime will appear merely repellent to the unrefined person', Deleuze understands the preparation of culture to precede the development of moral ideas. In other words, on his reading, Kant's position is that culture prepares humans to experience the sublime in order that they may develop morality (and thereby become free). When Deleuze writes that culture is the 'movement' of the genesis of aesthetic common sense, he means that as one becomes cultivated, one's experience of the sublime is enriched. The feeling of the sublime is what engenders aesthetic common sense, so cultivation is the starting point and initial impetus of the process. This cultivation can happen in many ways and be derailed in many more. Indeed, in a broad sense, everyone is cultivated since everyone develops habits that condition their experiences and ways of interpreting the world. Critique is the possibility of a certain kind of cultivation in revolutionary attunement. Of course, as is typically the case, while the accounts of culture in *Difference and Repetition* and in *Kant's Critical Philosophy* agree about its definition and place, there is an important difference as well. In the earlier text, Deleuze emphasises how culture prepares humans for the feeling of the sublime, which in turn prepares them for the moral law. It is the faculty of taste, properly cultivated, that allows the experience of the sublimity of Nature to be experienced as a symbol of the suprasensible. Since the faculty of taste was always latent within humans and only needed to be drawn out by proper cultivation, what this capacity to feel the suprasensible shows is that it is our human destiny to develop morality. In *Difference and Repetition*, on the other hand, the system of culture is determined by thought's highest form, which is in turn determined by critique. Since critique is immanent, it is not determined by any particular goal or destiny beyond that of 'breaking with *doxa*' – in other words, finding a 'way out' by creating something new. So, while both accounts of culture are not perfectly equivalent, their shared sense of 'culture' as the principle of the genesis of experiencing sublimity/ encounter and as philosophical training points to another level of agreement – on the practice of critique itself as the preparatory education of sensibility for encounter.

The means by which this is possible is as follows: though critique does not create knowledge, it does pose problems. The subject takes these problems up through the 'fractured I's' passive syntheses, which are passive not merely as the power of experiencing affections but as the power of habituation (or 'contemplation-contraction' (DR 87)). Habit, the vehicle through which the problems posed through the practice of critique shape the passive syntheses, is the 'powerlessness which is indistinguishable from the greatest power' (DR 147). The activity of thought applies to a passive subject, which 'experiences its effect rather than initiates it and which lives it like an Other within itself' (DR 86). This should recall the story of subjectivity as habituation that Deleuze develops in his reading of Hume, but it should also recall his account of dramatisation, which anticipates his development of critique.[15] Through the process of dramatisation, Ideas turn us 'into larvae' that 'bear Ideas in their flesh', radically reshaping that flesh (DR 272). Dramatisation harnesses the power of Ideas to alter habits at the level of the passive syntheses. In this sense, dramatisation is reminiscent of Bergson's 'fabulation' as 'an ominous power to create fictive visions so vivid and haunting that they may regulate behaviour'.[16] Similarly, when Hume speaks of an act of the mind he means that the mind is 'activated' (ES 26). Habituation creates the self passively. Culture, or *paideia*, prepares the soul for the experience of art, of encounter via habitualised critical practice. Hence the importance of the theory of time that fractures the I in the constitution of subjectivity. Subjectivity – and more importantly the contestation of subjectivity that opens one to encounters – is essentially linked with practice. Indeed, for Deleuze, the problem can only be correctly raised at the level of practice. Habits, practised over time, passively generate the self. It is important that this practice is one that, like drama, is based on stories rather than 'truth'. If subjects are the habit of making habits, the practice of critique creates new habits based on a non-Image of thought. It is only thus that critique cultivates open-mindedness, vulnerability and the intensification of the event that allows the selection of the active, affirmative forces and an appreciation for what is salient in unanticipatable moral dilemmas. Developing sensitivity to the affect happens through the freeing of the molecular, or becoming-woman/minor/imperceptible. This is the very same development that allows one to resist totalitarianism and the implicit notion of authenticity.

It is important to distinguish at this level the experience of art from the aesthetic more generally. Art is the capture of forces, the framing, as Sholtz says, of a moment of life. However, the aesthetic is the realm of the sensible, the passive syntheses, and perceptions. The affirmation of life and the capability of experiencing art as a rupture rather than as repellent cannot happen solely through intentionality – it requires a new sensibility. Critical thinking must include art encounters – with visual arts like painting, photography and cinema, linguistic arts like poetry, drama and journalism, auditory arts like music, kinetic arts like dance and theatre, as well as folk arts like storytelling, quilting and even cooking. For Deleuze, the movement from the passive synthesis of time to the active syntheses of memory, imagination and thought is not unidirectional but a spiral. It happens in the middle, not beginning with critique or with art, but in their relationship. As Sholtz acknowledges, 'engaging the artwork might not be enough, but it is a beginning, another beginning'.[17] Learning and instinct, Deleuze argues, can be understood according to the combinations and repetitions 'of active syntheses with passive syntheses' (DR 78). It is in the repetition – the making habitual – of the thinking about the thinking about art that the critical consciousness and the affirmative sensibility is activated. The contemplation/contraction of habit in the passive synthesis draws something new out of the repetition – and this something new is the ethos or form of life of questioning itself. Ethics is the intensity of a practice, the intensity of the integrative act of critique. Critical analysis uncovers the unconscious, setting philosophy the project of the cultivation of creativity, which manifests as an attitude of openness and affirmation. This is the meaning of the *amor fati*: not so much a reformulation of the Stoic ethics of self-mastery but a matter, as Sholtz says, of 'a more honest relationship with the ebbs and flows of the earth'.[18]

Notes

1. Deleuze chooses to call his own philosophical approach in *Difference and Repetition* 'transcendental empiricism' rather than 'critique', but the distinction between the two is primarily verbal. While Deleuze sees serious flaws in the way Kant deployed critique, he is unequivocally

convinced of the power and value of the immanent critical practice itself.
2. Eugene Holland, *Deleuze and Guattari's Anti-Oedipus*, New York: Routledge, 2002, p. viii.
3. Ibid. p. 35.
4. Kerslake, 'Deleuze, Kant, and the Question of Metacritique', p. 496.
5. Gilles Deleuze, 'On Spinoza', Lectures by Gilles Deleuze, at http://deleuzelectures.blogspot.com/2007/02/on-spinoza.html (accessed 1 February 2018).
6. Joe Hughes, 'Schizoanalysis and the Phenomenology of Cinema', in *Deleuze and the Schizoanalysis of Cinema*, ed. Ian Buchanan and Patricia MacCormack, London: Continuum, 2008, p. 16.
7. Kant claims in a letter to Herz that 'none of my critics understood me and the main questions as well as Herr Maïmon does', and in the same letter goes into great detail discussing Maïmon's 'most subtle investigations' ('To Marcus Herz, May 26, 1789', in Immanuel Kant, *Correspondence*, Cambridge: Cambridge University Press, 2007, pp. 311–12).
8. Janae Sholtz, *The Invention of a People*, Edinburgh: Edinburgh University Press, 2015, pp. 135, 116, 248.
9. Ibid. p. 259.
10. Ibid. p. 276.
11. Ibid. p. 85.
12. Ibid. p. 228.
13. 'Culture' is a translation of both the German words *Kultur* and *Bildung*. The late eighteenth century in Germany marked a period of heightened interest in the idea of culture, with particularly heated debate between Kant and Johann Herder surrounding the meaning of the term. See John Zammito's chapter on 'The *Aufklarung* of the 1760s: "Philosophy for the World" or *Bildung* as "Emancipation"', in his *Kant, Herder and the Birth of Anthropology* (Chicago: University of Chicago Press, 2002) for a fine exposition of the context leading up to this debate.
14. The debate between Herder and Kant can be centred on this question of the human telos. While Kant's understanding of *Bildung/Kultur* is grounded in a teleology structured toward practical ends, Herder's is non-teleological and based in an ever-expanding anthropology where different forms of culture develop different faculties within humans, none of which are higher or lower than the others. Like facets of a diamond, for Herder different forms of culture reveal different capacities of humanity.
15. For an excellent dive into this idea, see Didier Debaise's analysis of dramatisation, which he argues aims to show that 'all the notions developed in "The Method of Dramatisation" – such as the transformation of the status of Ideas, the first development of a theory of individuation,

the de-centering of subjectivity, the critique of representation – are part of one general function: to grant events the importance they call for. If a method is required for such an endeavour, it is because thought must become the site of the maximal intensification of what – beyond a psychological or anthropological point of view – is of importance.' Debaise, 'The Dramatic Power of Events', p. 5.
16. Sholtz, *The Invention of a People*, p. 239.
17. Ibid. p. 259.
18. Ibid. p. 238.

PART II

Critique as an Ethos – A Handbook for a Way Out

4

Critical Ethos

Ethos

The *Oxford English Dictionary* defines *ethos* as 'the characteristic spirit of a people, community, culture, or era as manifested in its attitudes and aspirations'. The verb form is *ethó*, which means 'to be accustomed', or, to have a behaviour or disposition fixed by habit.[1] It was a popular expression in ancient Greek philosophy and was made particularly influential through Aristotle's *Rhetoric*. It remained in circulation in the Renaissance humanists' discourses surrounding education, as it marked the distinction between the holistic approach of rhetoric and the more exclusively logical approach defined by dialectical *logos*. While the term remained part of the scholarly lexicon, Pierre Hadot has argued that its usage within philosophical ethics (despite the latter term itself being derived from ethos) waned in the West following the rise of Christianity.[2] The particular practices associated with the *ethoi* of the ancient philosophical schools were appropriated by the Christian monastic orders and subordinated to revealed theology.[3] Following the rise of the modern natural sciences, the *ethoi* of the ancient schools were not recuperated, although they did reappear in the works of Montaigne, Spinoza, Rousseau, Goethe, Thoreau and Nietzsche. Partly as a result of Hadot's work from the 1970s through the early 2000s, the notion of ethos began regaining popularity in philosophical scholarship as way of characterising the difference between ancient approaches to philosophy built on spiritual exercises that entangle theory with practice, and modern approaches that take ontology, epistemology and ethics to be fundamentally different fields that do not necessarily implicate one's very being or way of living. For Hadot, ancient philosophies such as Stoicism, Epicureanism and Platonism cannot be understood without an appreciation of their aim to cultivate certain dispositions toward existence through a deepening understanding of the role of the human in the cosmos. For the ancients, one became a philosopher as a result of an existential choice (or calling), one that brought with it a commitment to live a specific style of life. This is in sharp contrast with most modern philosophies, which in developing their discourse demand only one's intellectual assent, if that. From Hadot's point of view, the modern conception of philosophy has emptied it of its real power – its ability to nourish spiritual and intellectual growth.

The rising popularity of the notion of ethos as a corrective to philosophy understood as an abstract, academic subject rather than a 'way of life' has given rise to numerous new and fascinating works.[4] However, these have been largely focused on developing a complement to ethical theories that seek general principles of justice in theories of the human, the Good, or practical reason rather than discovering a replacement for them. For example, in *The Ethos of a Late-Modern Citizen*, Stephen White argues that an exploration of ethos as one's 'manner of being' or 'spirit' is necessary to adequately sustain the general principles discovered in universalising moral theories.[5] In contrast, the Deleuzian critical ethos resists adopting particular conceptions of the human, the Good, or reason, as these presuppositions inevitably serve agendas of domination by blinding ethicists to unanticipated features of moral salience. Instead, the Deleuzian critical ethos favours exploring ways of developing moral sensibilities that do not require guidance from general principles derived from such presuppositions. This theme is visible in an inchoate form throughout Deleuze's oeuvre. However, its explicit formulation owes much to Foucault's work from the 1980s.

In his essay 'What is Enlightenment?', Foucault explicitly links Kantian critique with the Greek notion of ethos. He begins by drawing attention to the originality of Kant's conception of his own present. Foucault argues that Kant conceives of his present, the Enlightenment, as a 'way out' – both as a process that releases us from our state of immaturity and as 'an act of courage' in which we leave behind the comforts of authority and put our own Reason to work (WE 306). For Foucault, the moment when one begins to reason for oneself is the moment when critique is most necessary, 'since its role is that of defining the conditions under which the use of Reason is legitimate in order to determine what can be known, what must be done, and what may be hoped' (WE 308). Once the responsibility for using one's own Reason has been taken, critique is necessary in order to guide Reason to the best decisions. Critique, on Foucault's reading, is the 'handbook' for a 'way out' (WE 305). From the Enlightenment perspective, it is only after the legitimate uses of Reason have been defined that 'autonomy can be assured' (WE 308).

Critical Ethos

Not only does Foucault call the Enlightenment the 'age of critique', he suggests re-conceiving it as an 'attitude' of critique rather than a period of history (WE 309). By 'attitude' he means:

> a mode of relating to contemporary reality; a voluntary choice made by certain people; in the end, a way of thinking and feeling; a way, too, of acting and behaving that at one and the same time marks a relation of belonging and presents itself as a task. A bit, no doubt, like what the Greeks called an ethos. (WE 309)

In other words, for Foucault, Enlightenment exists as an attitude or ethos that expresses a relationship to oneself defined by critique. Foucault believes that what connects modern subjects to the Enlightenment is a 'philosophical ethos that could be described as a permanent critique of our historical era' (WE 312). He goes on to claim that this philosophical ethos is a 'limit-attitude' (WE 315). The critique cannot be *for* or *against* the Enlightenment since it is an ethos that expresses a permanent critique of oneself as an historical artefact in so far as it is an evaluation of the limits of Reason. Foucault considers transforming the 'critique conducted in the form of necessary limitation into a practical critique that takes the form of a possible crossing-over' (WE 315). What defines one's own present is imagining it otherwise than it is, and transforming it not by destroying it but by grasping it in what it is. This is precisely what Deleuze does in his reading of Kantian critique. The ethos defined by critique necessitates a permanent evaluation and creation of oneself (limit/transgression-attitude). It would be not merely descriptive but practical, taking its goal to be resisting the presuppositions and habituated forms of experience that constrain life. As Foucault elegantly puts it:

> The critical ontology of ourselves has to be considered not, certainly, as a theory, a doctrine, nor even as a permanent body of knowledge that is accumulating; it has to be conceived as an attitude, an ethos, a philosophical life in which the critique of what we are is at one and the same time the historical analysis of the limits that are imposed on us and an experiment with the possibility of going beyond them. (WE 319)

In other words, this critical ethos of that necessitates self-evaluation and creation through historical analyses of external as well as internal limits defines a philosophical way of living that permanently seeks autonomy, understood as a searching 'beyond' the limits imposed on bodies.

Foucault's essay was written many years after Deleuze's *Difference and Repetition*, but it explicitly develops the very point of view that operates implicitly throughout Deleuze's oeuvre. Years prior to writing 'What is Enlightenment?', Foucault made similar points about Deleuze and Guattari's *Anti-Oedipus* in his Preface to that work. He reads that text as offering an 'ethics', a 'life style', and a 'way of thinking and living' that recalls Hadot's notion of ethos and anticipates his own reading of Kantian critique in the Enlightenment essay. The 'art of living counter to all forms of fascism' that Foucault finds in *Anti-Oedipus* could just as well be the transgressive limit-attitude that he discovers in Kantian critique (AO xiii). For Foucault, Deleuze and Guattari's 'manual or guide to everyday life' even includes a set of seven 'principles' for the development of autonomy: 1) Resist totalising paranoia in political action. 2) Resist hierarchisation in favour of proliferation, juxtaposition and disjunction. 3) Resist the categories of the negative in favour of what is positive and multiple. 4) Resist sadness in favour of desire's productivity as what has revolutionary force. 5) Resist grounding practice in Truth in favour of using practice to intensify and multiply thought. 6) Resist the sedimentation of the individual complicit in 'rights' discourse in favour of de-individualising bodies. And 7) 'Do not become enamoured of power' (AO xiii–xiv). While Foucault seemed content to formulate these ideas in term of 'principles', as expressions of an immanent notion of ethos they might be best understood in terms of Hadot's spiritual exercises, or perhaps as Deleuzo–Guattarian practices of *paideia*.

Paideia

In the Greek context, *paideia* was the core system of educational practices designed to reflect and develop the *ethoi* of the ancient philosophical schools alongside those of Athenian democracy and ideals of civic duty. In *What is Grounding?*, Deleuze defines Plato's understanding of *paideia* as 'The education of an ideal member of the polis' (WG 112). In *Nietzsche and Philosophy*, he applies this notion to Nietzsche's early work on culture in the *Untimely Meditations* (1876). There, Nietzsche contrasts the then-current German educational system's creation of 'cultural philistines' with a new, historically informed approach to education that would create genuinely cultured artists, philosophers and 'great individuals' (NP 138). Deleuze likewise uses the notion of *paideia* in *Difference and Repetition* to distinguish two different educational approaches: Approaches based on 'method' imply an intentional and calculated plan, a 'premeditated decision' that assumes the good will of the thinker while smuggling the dogmatism of common sense into thought via the plan's fixed outcome objectives and assessment techniques (NP 108). Approaches based on *paideia*, on the other hand, do not presume to know how or even what the thinker will learn but instead offer an immersive training that involves intensive exposure to the native conditions of thought while remaining open to what that produces. In other words, whereas method offers a recipe for thinking that can only reproduce itself, *paideia* is an investment of self in the process of becoming a thinker that can produce freedom and creativity. As Deleuze writes, 'there is no more a method for learning than there is a method for finding treasures' (DR 165). In *Twilight of the Idols*, Nietzsche associates the *paideia* of 'learning to *think*' that the Germans lack with the practice of logic as a craft – like dancing, but 'with concepts'.[6] The native conditions of thought can be absorbed and internalised through immersion in the 'craft' of logic and the study of history. In Deleuze, a similar story unfolds. *Paideia* appears in *Difference and Repetition* in the context of describing an 'education of the senses' that facilitates the movement of encounter from one faculty to the next (DR 165). This education or cultivation of sensibility does not have a 'method' but is a 'violent training' or 'involuntary adventure' that 'affects the entire individual' (DR 165). *Paideia* is an absorbing engagement with learning to think that implicates the individual through their bodily practices, unconscious evaluations and intentional analyses. As Deleuze describes it in *Nietzsche and Philosophy*, *paideia* involves a 'selective violence' (NP 109). As in language immersion training (when the language to be learned is used exclusively), *paideia* selects the immanent, legitimate forces to be used exclusively and follows their unfolding to the point of the individual's own deterritorialisation. It is to Deleuze's credit that he does not back down from describing this immersion as a violently vertiginous experience, one to which the apprentice thinker must submit in order to uncover the deep mystery of how suffering forges the new.[7] Here, in other words, the native conditions of thought into which *paideia* must immerse the thinker are the practices of critique. Critique, understood not as a set of rules or a method but as an ethos, is the underlying set of practices and values on which the *paideic* training is built.

What has been in the background of this reading of Deleuze's use of critique in *Difference and Repetition* are the two ideals he proposes for doing philosophy: the destruction of breaking with *doxa* and the creation of generating thought. These two moments are in effect two different faces of the critical practice itself. The first moment, which prepares the ground for the production of a thought without Image, is the radical critique of the dogmatic Image of thought. The second moment is the non-teleological critique of the limits and powers of the faculties. In describing how these two moments are lived, Deleuze introduces two characters: the Russian idiot and the Apprentice.

The radical critique of the dogmatic Image of thought puts into question all presuppositions, all ready-made answers, everything that is considered 'given'. Deleuze writes that:

> a philosophy which would be without any kind of presuppositions ... would take as its point of departure a radical critique of [the dogmatic Image of thought] ... a rigorous struggle against this Image ... As a result, it would discover its authentic repetition in a thought without Image, even at the cost of the greatest destructions and the greatest demoralisations, and a philosophical obstinacy with no ally but paradox. (DR 132)

The radical critique Deleuze is proposing obstinately questions everything – even to the point of demoralisation and de-individuation.[8] If what Deleuze is resisting in the dogmatic Image is its origin in morality and its consequences for freedom, perhaps this can be pushed further to the idea that radical critique does not just risk demoralisation/de-individuation but produces them as its goal. The persona Deleuze identifies as the 'Russian idiot' provokes the demoralisation by denying what 'everybody knows' or what 'cannot be denied': common sense (DR 130). Idiocy, Deleuze claims, is a sort of modesty that does not want to be represented or to represent anything. But this denial is also an expression of ill will and of an inability to think according to the standards set by the 'culture of the times', not of a good will and a natural capacity for thought. The philosopher 'takes the side' of the idiot because the idiot performs the critique of the dogmatic Image through her recalcitrance. The idiot is the one who can 'effectively begin and effectively repeats' (DR 130). However, this is a dangerous role to play in so far as the lack of presuppositions is only apparent. The idiot does not get beyond presuppositions – though they are intensely questioned. This is why Deleuze specifies that when the philosopher risks playing the idiot, it should be done 'in the Russian manner':

> that of an underground man who recognises himself no more in the subjective presuppositions of a natural capacity for thought than in the objec-

tive presuppositions of a culture of the times, and lacks the compass with which to make a circle. Such a one is the Untimely, neither temporal nor eternal. Ah Shestov, with the questions he poses, the ill will he manifests, the powerlessness to think he puts into thought and the double dimension he develops in these demanding questions concerning at once both the most radical beginning and the most stubborn repetition. (DR 130)

Deleuze is referring here to Lev Shestov, a fascinating and iconoclastic scholar of Russian and Jewish descent whose revolutionary ideas led him to a life of wandering as he clashed with one authority after another. His final magnus opus, *Athens and Jerusalem* (1938), which is the culmination of his fragmentary and aphoristic interpretations of Tolstoy, Dostoyevsky, Nietzsche and Kierkegaard, calls for the rejection of reason by philosophy. By associating Shestov with the persona of the idiot, Deleuze is suggesting that idiocy means iconoclasty and a determination to question what is considered rational and beyond question. It is not just a scholarly pursuit, but a way of living philosophy as a struggle against presuppositions. It is a way of living critically, 'in the Russian manner' (DR 130). This way of living has its own *paideia* of breaking with *doxa*: it is precisely the kind of preliminary training philosophers do: wide and careful reading, dogged questioning, dissenting interpretation, recursive problematising and dialogic argumentation. Consistent with the point of view of *paideia*, this philosophical culture is not a set of discrete skills but an immersion in looking at the world with wonder that makes the practice of asking 'why?' (or 'who?' or 'how?') an unshakeable habit. It means training in being able to think differently and against the persuasive initial positions presented by common sense, knowledge and morality. It is not just about critically evaluating others, but at the deepest level demands an ability to critically evaluate oneself and one's habits of thought.

The radical critique of the dogmatic Image dramatically personified by the Russian idiot clears the ground for the encounter and the process of producing a thought without Image. It frees the faculties from the burden of having to conform to common sense. It is analogous to the spiritual metamorphosis Nietzsche describes in *Thus Spoke Zarathustra*, which transforms the camel into the lion. While the camel 'carries the weight of established values', the lion 'destroys statues, tramples burdens, and leads the critique of all established values' (PI 53). But the lion is not the end of the story. There is another metamorphosis within which 'the lion must become child' (PI 53). This final metamorphosis, which 'represents play and a new beginning', is at least partially analogous to the second character Deleuze offers for understanding how the creation of a thought without Image occurs: the Apprentice (PI 53). If the Russian idiot personifies radical critique's destruction of the dogmatic Image of thought, the Apprentice personifies the role of non-teleological critique in thought's creative eluding of sedimentation into a new Image.

When a non-teleological critique evaluates each faculty for its intrinsic power, it describes a movement wherein the violence of a fundamental encounter on the level of sensibility acts as a spark to the fuse of thinking. The encounter plunges each faculty in its turn into an involuntary adventure in which the faculty 'is born to the extreme point of its dissolution' through a triple violence (DR 140–1). Deleuze's model of the Apprentice illustrates how such a critique is lived.

The Apprentice is 'someone who constitutes and occupies practical or speculative problems as such', living immersed in a philosophical, critical culture (DR 164). What the Apprentice does – learning – is not knowing.[9] Whereas knowledge means being in possession of rules that enable solutions (DR 164), learning means constituting 'the space of an encounter with signs, in which the distinctive points renew themselves in each other, and repetition takes shape while disguising itself' (DR 23). If the *paideia* of radical, destructive critique cultivates the open-mindedness and anti-fascist sensitivity that clears the space for an encounter, then the non-teleological critique's evaluation of the intrinsic power of the faculties sets in motion an 'exploration' of the Ideas each faculty produces as distinctive points in the wake of the encounter's rupture. The Apprentice seeks and becomes riveted to the encounter, treating it as a problem to be unpacked, taken apart, turned over, tasted, touched and tested. Each Idea, as the distinctive expression of the faculty's power at its limit, is taken as an object and thus transmits the rupture from one faculty to the next.[10] As Deleuze writes, 'the exploration of Ideas and the elevation of each faculty in its transcendent exercise amounts to the same thing. These are two aspects of an essential apprenticeship or process of learning' (DR 164). When the Apprentice experiences the encounter, the attempt to explore and grasp the insensible (the Idea produced by sensibility at its limit) leads imagination to produce the unimaginable at its limit, which sparks memory to produce the unrememberable, and then thought to generate the unthinkable – a thought without Image. The Apprentice raises each faculty to its

Critical Ethos

transcendent exercise by trying to grasp in each faculty what is its alone (exploring its distinctive Idea as an object) and thereby transmits the violence of the encounter from one faculty to the next. Each faculty thus discovers its unique power and limit, but also its difference and its repetition. For instance, the faculty of thought, when confronted with what it alone is capable of grasping, finds its distinctive difference. But when thought is confronted with what is unthinkable it instantaneously engenders the repetition of thinking. The shock of the unthinkable becomes a bodily sensation that encourages the repetition of encounter. This is the education of the senses. Of course, this happens only as long as the critique undertaken is non-teleological. When it is, the evaluation of the faculties' intrinsic power or limits is independent of how that power could be used for any pre-established end. This allows for the 'exploration of Ideas' to proceed as a play that unites difference to difference without a goal, ideal or *telos*. This frees learning to be creative and its repetition to become a spiral, rather than stagnating into a simple cycle.[11] Repetition as a cycle represents the possession of knowledge, which is derivative and produces the same rather than the new. Repetition as a spiral takes shape in an unfolding process, following a line that loops around a central encounter as it simultaneously speeds into the future, disguising its own genesis in its continual turning into new beginnings.[12] As Kristensen writes, 'learning is not mediated by reason but by an ethical ethos about creation of possibilities of life'.[13]

In this way the Apprentice keeps the Russian idiot's destruction of dogmatism from sedimenting into a new Image. Apprenticeship dramatises both a lived subordination to the process of learning and the perpetuation of non-mastery. Neither the Russian idiot nor the Apprentice get 'beyond' presuppositions. The Russian idiot contests them while the Apprentice selects, problematises and follows the forces uncovered in that contestation, disallowing those forces from becoming new Images of thought as knowledge. The 'critical ethos' dramatised in these personae force a constant re-evaluation of learning that has become sedimented into knowledge. It is an Apprenticeship in Russian idiocy: the eternal ungrounding of thought by thought. This is an intentional practice, but even more so a clarification of the power of a thought without Image to resist setting up a new Image of thought. It is thus that the figures of the Russian idiot and the Apprentice can be interpreted as practical personae modelling a way of living Deleuze's critical philosophy. This model resists the folding of encounter back into the dogmatic Image of thought. But it also answers the question of what preparatory education is necessary to be able to grasp the revolutionary potential in the encounter. Without any kind of critical ethos, the encounter might arrive while the thinker looks right past it, unable to perceive in it what is so unique and resistant to recognition. As Levi Bryant writes, 'thought requires an apprenticeship or training in signs to engender an openness to the encounter, to prevent it from covering over the difference which manifests itself with the subjects and objects resulting from the syntheses of habitus'.[14] 'Openness' to the encounter means not only an open-mindedness to perceive it, but also the willingness to seek it out in the world, in one's habits of interpretation and experience, and in the ways of living one presupposes. This critique is not just a *cogitere aude* or a daring to think. It is a daring to *not* know, a daring to learn. Cultivation through living philosophical critique opens individuals to the experience of the encounter by giving them tools for generating thought and breaking with *doxa*.

But the story does not end here. There is a final figure in this drama of living the critical ethos that is crucial for the preparatory education of the senses for the encounter. This final lived figuration of the critical ethos is one that Deleuze only considers after having written *Difference and Repetition*: becoming-woman. While not a persona in the sense that the Russian idiot and Apprentice were, becoming-woman nonetheless dramatises an essential aspect of the critical ethos. In *a Thousand Plateaus*, becoming-woman is presented as possessing a 'special introductory power' for the process of becoming (TP 248). It is 'the key to all the other becomings'; as such, every movement beyond the normative begins and must pass through a becoming-woman (TP 277). This is because 'woman' is the dominant form against which the masculine, majoritarian molar form has been defined. As Rosi Braidotti has argued, the adoption of the female perspective for feminist resistance uncovers and puts into question all the dominant, masculine political structures that tend to stagnate life's productivity. This aspect of the critical ethos is an important step beyond what the Russian idiot and Apprentice offered. As Sholtz explains:

> implicit to the concept of dramatisation is an ethico-aesthetic imperative to counteractualise ourselves as a necessary precursor to entering into processes of dramatisation or engaging on the level of affective interaction on the plane of immanence. In other words, dramatisation as counteractualisation includes the paradoxical imperative for individuals to de-individualise themselves so as to engage the virtual elements of the event.[15]

Unlike the Russian idiot, who questions presuppositions, and unlike the Apprentice, who plays with Ideas, the process of becoming-woman is affective, bodily, and requires inhabiting uncomfortable, vulnerable perspectives. Becoming-woman is the counteractualisation of the individual. It destabilises the monopoly that identity-based thinking has on production and desire. It celebrates the multiplicity of desires by focusing not on the ways abstract norms and identities are represented but rather on the way in which every lived gesture repeats a series of images and, in so doing, remakes those images anew.

Much of the literature surrounding Deleuze and Guattari's story of becoming-woman has questioned its motives, its possible subterranean privileging of male perspectives, and its power of real change.[16] The most serious of these objections can be summarised in the following question: To what extent can 'becoming-woman' serve to empower women and minorities, given the historical lack of strong identities that have been available to them to facilitate their becoming?[17] On Braidotti's reading, the fight for equality justifies the practice of minoritarian identity politics. The more important question is what happens when nomadic minorisations are ignored. On Pelagia Goulimari's reading, 'a dialectic of appropriation and exclusion in relation to minoritarian movements within and outside of feminism marks both texts ... [with appropriation and exclusion being] a side effect of rejecting the concept of the "becoming minoritarian" in favour of "sexual difference" feminism'.[18] Unlike Braidotti, Goulimari reads becoming-woman as connected to becoming-minor. This reading is more in line with the spirit of becoming-woman in *A Thousand Plateaus*. In a creative re-reading of Beauvoir's 'one is not born, but rather becomes, a woman',[19] Deleuze and Guattari write that even the woman 'has to become-woman' (TP 275). This happens through the process of marginalisation in patriarchal society. Becoming-woman thus acts as the doorway into the rhizomatic theatre of becoming in so far as it signals a willingness to inhabit perspectives, situations and desires other than those currently valued as powerful, not just the perspective of women. Becoming-woman is critical for deterritorialising not just patriarchal binary oppositions, but all normalisations and molar categories. Becoming-woman is thus not an end in itself, but plays an introductory role that may facilitate a potentially infinite number of 'minoritarian' becomings.

As Sholtz has convincingly argued, the politics of identity that Braidotti and others have defended should be rethought in favour of a more thoroughgoing schizoanalysis of becoming-woman that is not exclusionary but attempts to reject all normalisation and power.[20] Sholtz calls her model, which should set up a great deal of new thinking, 'intersectional transversality'. Indeed, the evolution that feminism has undergone is a perfect model for the way to approach the critical ethos: after making an interpretation and living it to the fullest, revise it and move forward based on greater openness, flexibility and connectedness in order to avoid the trap of sedimenting into dogmatism. Such a schizoanalysis, or minor critique, would also be a war machine – a crucial companion to the concept of nomadology. The concept of the war machine was derived from Paul Virilio, and in Deleuze and Guattari it refers to the aggregation of a series of phenomena that produce 'war', the outcomes of which can be 'radical de-stabilisation, de-territorialisation, de-subjectification and even de-identification' – a result of the war machine's alliance with the nomad in clashes with the state. 'Denuding' the concept of 'war' of its military connotations entirely, Paul Patton, as Rick Dolphijn puts it, 'reads the war machine as a machine of metamorphosis, giving an insight into how this concept should be used and revealing nomadology, with the war machine of metamorphosis as its tool, as an *anti-semiology* aimed at decoding whatever strategies it is confronted with'.[21] Thus the Russian idiot is reinscripted toward the revolutionary critique of the faculties' limits and powers. The war machine is a politicised Russian idiot, wielding an inability to understand norms to the point of their destruction. This, of course, hearkens back to the concept of dramatisation from Deleuze's early works, which was utilised in *Difference and Repetition* to develop the personae of the Russian idiot and the Apprentice as forces of critique acting against the sedimentation of thought.

In summary, the Russian idiot destroys dogmatism, the Apprentice explores Ideas as pure play, and becoming-woman models a lived deterritorialisation of norms, de-individuating the body and its habits of thought in a political movement. These represent the three facets of the critical ethos: radical, non-teleological and minor, adding the figure of the nomad to the Nietzschean figures of the lion and the child. Their imperative forms are: dare to not know, dare to learn and dare to grow.

Vulnerability

Deleuze's ideal of philosophy as breaking with *doxa* acknowledges the necessity of evaluating every starting point, every presupposition and every habit, especially those that bear the form of common sense. Such an evaluation is the fundamental condition of philosophising. However, this evaluation cannot attain a point of view *beyond* presuppositions. Presuppositions – and indeed, the entire structure of recognition/representation – are constitutive of everyday experience and living. As such, it would be meaningless to get rid of them, like a plant cutting itself off from its own roots. Without presuppositions, neither consciousness, agency nor ethics would be possible, and the creation of new thoughts would cease. This includes the set of presuppositions encapsulated by the dogmatic Image of thought. Deleuze is preoccupied with this point from his earliest works. In *What is Grounding?* he is recorded as saying,

> Thought is entrained by a fundamental, inevitable illusion. It is not an illusion that indicates the reaction of our passions to thought, but the influence of thought on thought. For Descartes, the prejudice came from us not simply being thinking beings. The principle of illusion came from the body. Kant's idea is that pure thought falls into an illusion that is interior to it. Whence a 'transcendental' illusion and not an empirical illusion. Reason itself engenders the illusion into which it falls. Therefore it can never disappear. It is just necessary to prevent that it deceives us. This illusion belongs to the nature of reason. The dialectic is then at the same time the movement of the transcendental illusion and the consciousness of that illusion. (WG 110–11)

Like Kant's 'transcendental illusions', one cannot do without presuppositions even though they lead inevitably into error. But all is not lost. If there is no way to get definitively beyond presuppositions, the next best alternative is to adopt a critical attitude toward them. What this means is developing a critical attitude toward oneself, cultivating in oneself an openness – even a readiness – for encounter and thought. Becoming an idiot 'in the Russian manner' means cultivating a disposition of dogged questioning and scepticism. Becoming an Apprentice involves immersion in the play of Ideas unfurled in the encounter, without any pre-set goal or destination in mind. Becoming-woman entails cultivating a willingness to inhabit a life out of step with the norms that confer power, and seeing the privileges of molar identifications and majoritarian alignment for what they are: blockages of life to be dismantled. From his earliest description of critique, Deleuze has described the practice as the nearly paradoxical idea of the self-judging of Reason by Reason. This is the 'essential principle' of an 'immanent critique' (KCP 3). Critique is self-evaluation at the transcendental level of the faculties, the level of the presuppositions and habits that chain thinking to repetitions of the same. While Reason's inner conflict does play an important role in Deleuze's reading of Kant, it is not as the motivating force behind the necessity of philosophical inquiry. Rather, this inner conflict powers critique. It problematises through its self-evaluations. Though critique cannot get the individual beyond presuppositions, it can put those presuppositions in question and facilitate growth through its de-individualising practices. That is why critique is not a method once applied and done forever. It has to be a way of life or it does not work. If there is no 'beyond' presuppositions and habits for thinkers, their presuppositions and habits must always be evaluated, and as they re-form they must be evaluated again. Deleuze is hostile to the notion of method because a method implies a pre-established goal and a correct path to achieving it, effectively putting presuppositions into the very practice meant to eliminate them. This is why critique is not associated with method but with ethos, with the formative forces representing the ideal of philosophy itself. That is, the creation of a new habit of contesting habits.

Living in this way is not something that should start in one place or another. It is always in progress, and, if one chooses it, one joins in the middle. The radical critique dramatised by the Russian idiot refuses dogmatism by refusing to understand the terms of problems posed according to common-sense norms. The terms of the culture clash surrounding the 'proper' use of gendered public restrooms by people who identify as queer, trans or gender-non-conforming could be contested on the basis that they involve an illegitimate use of the transcendent, molar categories of sex and gender to regulate behaviour. This is a destruction of presuppositions at the root level. The non-teleological critique dramatised by the Apprentice's playful, immersive learning excludes the illegitimate defining of knowledge that limits thought's recursive power by selecting and affirming the Ideas that include the maximum of difference. Experiential education practices that immerse students in the voices and perspectives of diverse people, animals and even the earth and cosmos encourage the cultivation of empathy, growth and creative thinking while eluding the recreation of the canon of beliefs that tend to colonise students' ears, vision and minds. This is a play with Ideas that encourages the emergence of the unanticipatable. The minor critique dramatised by becoming-woman cultivates a lived appreciation of one's implicit biases, particularly those biases that conceal the limitations within one's own well-meaning projects. The intersectional challenge to traditional feminists' implicit reliance on white, Western models of women's experience revealed to many established feminists the limitations of their own perspectives and the necessity of actively promoting the inclusion of non-white, non-European, non-middle-class voices. This challenge to feminism is an auspicious model of what becoming-woman entails, for it does not mean trading one molar identification for another, one Image for another. This suggests that Deleuze's perspective is not immune from its own minor critique, its own becoming-woman as becoming-minor. As Barbara Gibson has argued, Deleuzians' Nietzschean prioritisation of the categories of independence and active becoming (rather than Deleuze and Guattari's rhizomatic notion of connectedness) should be subject to critique by problematising that vantage point as privileged and majoritarian in relation to bodies that have been marked as disabled.[22] The present text no doubt creates a perspective enmeshed in legitimate and illegitimate uses of the faculties and should also be held to the standard of becoming through encounters that frame new Ideas for exploration and self-critique. Importantly, the affective, bodily becoming undergone in the sincere questioning of one's own way of experiencing the world inevitably leads back to a further refusal to engage with the terms offered for problems posed according to common-sense norms. This is the recursivity of thought that cultivates the habit of resistance to habits and leads to genuine growth, even if that growth never fully and irrevocably frees one from all common-sense presuppositions.

The ethos developed here in tandem with Deleuze's critical practice can alternatively be described as set of characteristics in which certain virtues become habituated in the body. Though the vocabulary of virtues is fraught from a Deleuzian perspective, the idea, as Sholtz would put it, is 'too tantalizing' a thought not to explore. While Deleuzian virtues must be distinguished from moralistic virtues determined by the goal of subjugating bodies – for instance, the virtues of self-control, moderation, patience and chastity – there are others that the critical ethos encourages. These include, but are not limited to: open-mindedness, questioning, self-evaluation, connectivity, play, affirmation and creativity. Open-mindedness has been championed by William Hare as the 'readiness to consider new ideas coupled with the commitment to accept only those that pass scrutiny'.[23] This readiness operates as a sincere quest for new ways of thinking and perceiving. If this quest is not chosen, the individual risks stagnating, failing to ever grow or develop. Those who are open to perspectives that question their own develop a resistance to immediately reactionary responses, thus contributing to dialogue and productive moving forward. The virtue of connectivity – the simultaneous appreciation of one's dependence on history, on others, on the earth, and one's imbrication with all bodies, concepts and futures in the flow of becoming – fosters relationships built on responsiveness rather than the false ideal of atomistic independence. It encourages, as Ronald Bogue puts it, 'a mutual undoing of each other's initial understandings'.[24] While creativity and invention enrich living, pose unanticipatable questions, and operate as vehicles of encounter, dogmatic allegiance to knowledge blocks creative production. Play and affirmation, both expressions of the joy of living and the willingness to take chances, contribute to an attitude of productivity rather than lack. And play does not lack seriousness. As Foucault says, the Deleuzo-Guattarian militant knows it is not sadness that possesses revolutionary force, but the 'connection of desire to reality' that is not grounded in Truth but in a constant learning that intensifies thought by maximising difference (AO xiii–xiv). Similarly, affirmation is not affirmation of the negative but selection of the positive and productive. These virtues of open-mindedness, questioning, connectivity, creativity, play and affirmation do not hearken back to a 'golden mean' or the basic worth of prudence. Rather, they point to a fundamental imperative of living a Deleuzian critical ethos: cultivating vulnerability.

Appreciation for the importance of recuperating and expanding the notion of vulnerability has grown rapidly over the past two decades. This growth has issued in a myriad of challenges to a tradition in modern philosophy of understanding vulnerability as a weakness to be eradicated rather than an openness to connection. Onora O'Neill, for instance, argues that ethics should begin with a theory of agency as shared vulnerability.[25] Marina Berzins McCoy develops a minor reading of the Greeks in which vulnerability plays a significant role among the most important virtues.[26] Most importantly, Erinn Gilson persuasively redefines vulnerability not in terms of the 'negative', where it is 'equated with weakness, dependency, powerlessness, deficiency, and passivity' but with a positive 'epistemic' vulnerability that begins with 'being open to not knowing', 'being wrong', and cultivates a form of courage as the willingness to put oneself in uncomfortable situations, such as in confronting the implicit biases of one's own point of view or having to acknowledge the unintended racism, sexism or elitism in one's deeds.[27] Becoming-woman, becoming-animal and becoming-child all point to becoming vulnerable. They are the bodily, affective, concrete ways of trying to take the perspective of those who are disenfranchised, ignored or oppressed. The courage this kind of vulnerability takes leads back to another reading of Deleuze's claim about powerlessness in *Difference and Repetition*. If 'powerlessness is the greatest power', perhaps vulnerability is the greatest strength (DR 130)? This would be a deeper sense of strength than strength understood as power over others, or even as power over oneself. It would not be the might of domination but the courage to listen, to be implicated, and to change one's way of living as one continues learning and connecting difference to difference. Such a strength – a *virtu* in the Italian sense – would be the force of self-surpassing, of 'acquir[ing] consistency without losing the infinite into which thought plunges' (WP 42).

Much work remains to be done on developing the virtue of vulnerability, in particular the finer points of how to cultivate it as a dispositional habit. Before this work can be done, however, an important question intervenes, which has to do with the critical ethos itself. It is a fairly straightforward question that seeks to establish whether there might be implicit biases hidden within the Deleuzian ethos developed here. The question is this: Is the critical ethos presenting a new Image of thought rather than a non-Image of thought? Consistent with Foucault's suggestion that we locate the legacy of Kantian Enlightenment in the ethos defined by critique, Deleuze's critique must be evaluated as a 'handbook' for a 'way out' of the dogmatic Image of thought and its practical implications. Given the parallel between how Deleuze understands culture in *Difference and Repetition* and how he suggests Kant understands culture in *Kant's Critical Philosophy*, an evaluation of the extent to which Deleuze's critique breaks with the foundational anthropology and moral teleology of its Kantian antecedent is imperative.

Notes

1. Strong's Greek Lexicon, 1486.
2. Pierre Hadot, *Philosophy as a Way of Life*, Oxford: Blackwell, 1995. While Hadot is careful to acknowledge that several of the most influential early Christian apologists made the integration of Greek philosophy into the Christian 'style of life, spiritual attitude, and tonality' possible, by the time of the outlawing of the ancient schools in 529 CE, the Greek *ethoi* had ceased to exist as viable, independent ways of philosophical living (p. 129).

3. Pierre Hadot, *What is Ancient Philosophy?*, Cambridge, MA: Belknap Press, 2004.
4. See William McNeill's *The Time of Life: Heidegger and Ethos*, New York: SUNY Press, 2007; Stephen White's *The Ethos of a Late-Modern Citizen*, Cambridge, MA: Harvard University Press, 2009; Robert Nadeau's *Rebirth of the Sacred: Science, Religion, and the New Environmental Ethos*, Oxford: Oxford University Press, 2012; and Charles Taylor's *A Secular Age*, Cambridge: Harvard University Press, 2007; for excellent examples of this turn.
5. White, *The Ethos of a Late-Modern Citizen*, pp. 2–3.
6. Friedrich Nietzsche, *Twilight of the Idols and The Anti-Christ: or How to Philosophize with a Hammer*, trans. R. J. Hollingdale, London: Penguin Classics, 1990, pp. 76–7.
7. See Nietzsche, *On the Genealogy of Morals*, section 188, pp. 57–8.
8. For a nice discussion of individuation as the process by which one passes through the unconscious in order to attain consciousness, see Christian Kerslake's *Deleuze and the Unconscious*, London: Continuum, 2006.
9. The pedagogy of learning is not a question of the master bestowing pre-packaged knowledge or even drilling the Apprentice to produce the 'correct' answer. The pedagogy of learning is culture – understood as a violent training in evaluating presuppositions through a constant questioning, problematising and creating.
10. As McMahon has argued, treating Ideas as problems means that 'they confront and compel thought in virtue of their positive indeterminacy, an indeterminacy that nevertheless provokes thought to its highest powers of determination' (Melissa McMahon, 'Immanuel Kant', in *Deleuze's Philosophical Lineage*, ed. Graham Jones and Jon Roffe, Edinburgh: Edinburgh University Press, 2009, p. 96).
11. Knowledge can be applied, but learning is the creative process of confronting and muddling through a problem. Apprenticeship is directed to the future, not the past (see PS 26).
12. As Iain Mackenzie and Robert Porter have emphasised, the creation of concepts that learning as play models is a practical (rather than merely theoretical) activity. See 'Dramatisation as Method in Political Theory', *Contemporary Political Theory* 10:4 (2011), pp. 482–501.
13. Kristensen, 'Thinking Normativity in Deleuze's Philosophy', p. 18.
14. Bryant, *Difference and Givenness*, p. 77.
15. Janae Sholtz, 'Dramatisation as Life Practice', *Deleuze Studies* 10:1 (2016), p. 52.
16. See Louise Burchill, 'Becoming Woman: A Metamorphosis in the Present Relegating Repetition of Gendered Time to the Past', *Time & Society* 19 (March 2010), pp. 181–97, for an excellent response to these criticisms.
17. Jennifer Spiegel, 'Becoming Nomadic, Becoming Woman: Minoritarian

Becomings in the Deleuzian Theater', University of British Columbia doctoral thesis, 2005.
18. Pelagia Goulimari, 'Minoritarian Feminism? Things to Do with Deleuze and Guattari', *Hypatia* 14:2 (1999), p. 1481.
19. Simone de Beauvoir, *The Second Sex*, trans. Constance Borde and Sheila Malvoney-Chevallier, New York: Vintage, 2011, p. 283.
20. See Sholtz, 'Schizoanalysis and the Deterritorialisations of Transnational Feminism', in *Deleuze and the Schizoanalysis of Feminism*.
21. Rick Dolphijn, 'Nomadology', in *Encyclopedia of Identity*, ed. Ronald L. Jackson II, Los Angeles: SAGE, 2010, p. 508. Dolphijn is referring to Paul Patton, *Deleuze and the Political*, London: Routledge, 2000.
22. See Barbara Gibson, 'Disability, Connectivity and Transgressing the Autonomous Body', *Journal of Medical Humanities* 27:3 (2006), pp. 187–96, where Gibson draws on Deleuze and Guattari's reconfiguration of the static subject as active becoming to critique philosophies of activity that marginalise bodies normatively labelled as disabled.
23. William Hare, *Open-Mindedness and Education*, Montreal: McGill-Queens University Press, 1979, p. 52.
24. Ronald Bogue, *Deleuze's Way*, Burlington: Ashgate Publishing, 2007, p. 14.
25. Onora O'Neill, *Towards Justice and Virtue*, Cambridge: Cambridge University Press, 1996.
26. Marina Berzins McCoy, *Wounded Heroes: Vulnerability as a Virtue in Ancient Greek Literature*, Oxford: Oxford University Press, 2013.
27. Erinn Gilson, 'Vulnerability, Ignorance, and Oppression', *Hypatia* 26:2 (2011), p. 324. See also Gilson's *The Ethics of Vulnerability*.

5

Moral Destiny and Culture

What is most interesting about the Deleuzian practice of critique is that it is not a matter of moving beyond the presuppositions encapsulated by the dogmatic Image of thought, but of affirming them in their danger. Presuppositions cannot be eliminated, even though they subject one to conformity and rob one of one's power of thinking newness. Deleuze's solution is to subject our presuppositions to a critique that does not try to avoid them but to affirm them, to evaluate them according to the immanent conditions of their genesis, and create new forms of relationship to them. Such an affirmation is transformative in so far as it is recursively activated through the faculties' movement 'beyond' their limits. Though one cannot get definitively beyond the limits imposed by the subjective presuppositions of the dogmatic Image of thought, those limits can be affirmed by evaluating them as the grid through which ones sees the world. This affirmation can then reveal something about the world at the level of how social forces work through subjects. The 'education of the senses' described by Deleuze as *paideia* is informed by this destructive affirmation of presuppositions rather than by a theory of human nature, of the Good, or of practical reason.

Kant's Hidden Moralism

As was shown previously, on Deleuze's reading, Kant's position is that culture prepares humans to experience the sublime in order that they may produce morality. One implication of this reading is that culture is not only necessary for one's individual experience of the sublime – it is also necessary for the readiness with which anyone can expect their judgement concerning the sublime to be accepted by others. As culture increases, aesthetic common sense about the sublime becomes established. The feeling of the sublime is a subjective presupposition – 'which, however, we believe ourselves to be justified in demanding of everyone' (CJ §29) – that leads to the acknowledgment that there is an a priori principle of moral feeling within human beings. On Deleuze's reading of Kant, cultivation involves the development of what Kant alternately calls 'moral ideas' or 'moral feeling'. Even though moral feeling must be developed through culture, the a priori principle of moral feeling is the ground for the necessity of the assent individuals expect from other people concerning their own judgement on the sublime. Aesthetic common sense is established through the validity of the expectation of the experience of sublimity being recognisable to everyone, but in order for that expectation to form, culture must already have developed moral feeling in people. However, if culture is required for the moral feeling that makes individuals capable of experiencing sublimity, the experience of the sublime is limited to those who share the appropriate preparatory cultivation. So, there are actually two questions: the question of what counts as the appropriate preparatory cultivation, and the question of whether the validity of the aesthetic common sense is undermined. After all, aesthetic common sense is established through the validity of the expectation of the experience of sublimity being recognisable to everyone, not just to those who share the same culture.

Kant himself worries about the relationship between culture and the genesis of aesthetic common sense. His worry is that in requiring culture, the experience of sublimity may be taken as merely a matter of convention. In section 29 of the *Critique of Judgement* he tries to clarify that while the experience of the sublime requires culture, it is not generated by culture:

> But just because the judgement on the sublime in nature requires culture (more so than that on the beautiful), it is not therefore first generated by culture and so to speak introduced into society merely as a matter of convention; rather it has its foundation in human nature, and indeed in that which can be required of everyone and demanded of him along with healthy understanding, namely in the predisposition to the feeling for (practical) ideas, i.e., to that which is moral.

The analogy with seed cultivation introduced previously – in the explanation of Kant and his contemporaries' understanding of 'culture' – can be helpful in explaining what Kant means by claiming that culture is required for the experience of the sublime without the feeling of the sublime thereby becoming a matter of convention. If you sow seeds in the dust, many will die, some will be carried away to greener fields, and some will put down roots in the dust, growing stunted and lopsided. If you cultivate the dusty field by breaking up the hard earth and mixing the dust in with the clay and organic material buried beneath it, the loamy soil you develop will nourish and support the seeds' healthy growth and abundant production. The analogue of loamy soil for humans is the proper form of cultivation of moral feeling, while the seed is the faculty brought through culture 'to attend purposiveness' and thereby experience the sublime (CJ §29 'General remark on the exposition of the aesthetic reflective judgement'). 'Purposiveness' is the word most English translators use for Kant's concept of *Zweckmässigkeit*. Kant defines this term in section 10 of the *Critique of Judgement*, 'On Purposiveness in General', where he claims that purposiveness is 'the causality of a concept with respect to its object'. That is, 'purposiveness' is the quality by virtue of which an object is the end of a concept. The faculty of attending purposiveness is thus the capacity to see lawfulness in contingency. What happens in cultivation is that the capacity for attending purposiveness humans already had within them is developed, just as the dust is developed into loamy soil not by something extra being added to it but by drawing to the top the rich organic material beneath it. What is important for Kant's defence of the relationship between culture and common sense is that the faculty of attending purposiveness is not added onto the other human capacities like fertiliser is added to soil. That faculty lies dormant within humans until the proper form of cultivation awakens it. As Kant insists, moral feeling is part of 'human nature' just as 'healthy understanding' is (CJ §29).

The faculty that attends purposiveness is the faculty of taste. It is the faculty of perceiving in sensible Nature the imprint of the suprasensible. It judges those conditions immanent to sensible Nature that establish within it the capacity to express or symbolise something suprasensible. The beauty and sublimity of Nature symbolise the suprasensible and allow individuals to imagine a moral author of the world. It is the faculty of taste, properly cultivated, that allows individuals to perceive this symbolism. Thus Deleuze can write that, 'it is within this genesis [of aesthetic common sense] that we discover that which is fundamental to our destiny' (KCP 52). Human destiny turns out to be, unsurprisingly, the development of morality.

In the very short final section of *Kant's Critical Philosophy*, 'History or Realisation', Deleuze quickly introduces the ideas of history, 'unsocial sociability', 'the mechanism of forces' and 'the conflict of tendencies' by connecting them to ideas of culture, Reason's ends, man's moral destiny, Society and 'civil constitution' (KCP 74–5). The idea of 'unsocial sociability' is the key to understanding the connection between all of these ideas. 'Unsocial sociability' is Kant's term for the conflict between human beings' natural tendency to associate with others and their natural tendency to resist living socially. According to Kant's thinking in 'Idea for a Universal History with Cosmopolitan Intent' (1784), the conflict between these tendencies was ordained by Nature in order to bring about the cultivation of the faculties. In that work Kant likens the faculty of Reason to a 'seed' planted in human beings by Nature. Just like plant seeds require cultivation of the soil in order to grow and become fruitful, the faculty of Reason requires cultivation by 'trial, practice, and instruction in order gradually to progress from one level of insight to another' (IUH 'Second Thesis'). For Kant, Nature has its own form of species education. It is man's unsocial tendency that Nature uses as the means to cultivate Reason. It is, Kant claims, man's selfishness, 'heartless competitive vanity' and 'insatiable desire to possess and to rule' that 'awakens all his powers, brings him to conquer his inclination to laziness and, propelled by vainglory, lust for power, and avarice, to achieve a rank among his fellows whom he cannot tolerate but from whom he cannot withdraw' (IUH 'Fourth Thesis'). In other words, the violently unsocial desire of humans to direct everything according to their own ideas is the force behind the progress of their Reason. Culture is motivated by violence, vanity and desire.

This unsocial tendency poses a problem for social order. On the one hand, freedom is necessary for unsociability to flourish and thus force Reason to progress. On the other hand, that same unsocial tendency must be subdued by 'irresistible force' so that social order is maintained. Humans require masters, Kant writes, 'who will break [their] will and force [them] to obey' (IUH 'Sixth Thesis'). In his essay 'What is Enlightenment?', also written in 1784, Kant praises the Prussian ruler Frederick II whose 'well-disciplined, numerous army' allows him to say: 'Argue as much as you want and about what you want, but obey!'[1] Here, state-sanctioned violence is legitimate in so far as it is a means to the end of preserving social order – and hence state power. Of course, in 'Idea for a Universal History with Cosmopolitan Intent', Kant recognises the problem with his legitimation of state-sanctioned violence. The problem is that the master (in other words, the state) also needs a master, who in turn needs a master, who in turn needs a master. The true master and true end of Nature, what Kant calls the most difficult and final problem to be solved, is the creation of a perfectly just 'civil constitution' (IUH 'Fifth Proposition'). As Deleuze writes, 'the formation of a perfect civil constitution ... is the highest object of Culture, the end of history, or the truly terrestrial good sovereign' (KCP 74). Kant's reasoning is that only a civil constitution that is perfectly just could inspire the unfailing self-regulation of one's own unsocial tendency.[2] What is important is that, for Kant, this self-regulation is equivalent with morality. Morality is self-legislation in so far as morality is autonomy. And since morality is the highest level of insight it is possible to cultivate in Reason, morality is the truly *final* and *last* end of Reason and of Nature. The perfect civil constitution is the only milieu in which the moral destiny of man can be completed.

The same structure of a conflict that engenders social harmony holds at the level of the relations between faculties. The logic of violence and powerlessness that are internalised to create a new and greater power is repeated in the process of unsocial sociability. Moreover, the structure Deleuze identifies across Kant's oeuvre bears an uncanny resemblance to the Platonic micro-macro parallel between the proper governing of the soul and the proper governing of society. Deleuze writes: 'It is by the mechanism of forces and the conflict of tendencies (cf. "unsocial sociability") that sensible nature, in man himself, presides over the establishment of a Society, the only milieu in which a last end can be realised' (KCP 75). Deleuze's suggestion that we compare the conflict of tendencies and the mechanism of forces, as they work through 'man himself', with unsocial sociability invites the reader to connect the structure of the genesis of common sense with the structure of historical 'progress'. Thus Kant's account of unsocial sociability is connected to the discordant accord of faculties within what Deleuze sees as the organising principle of the whole of Kant's critical philosophy: the moral destiny of rational man.

At the core of Deleuze's reading is the idea that what Kant takes to be the proper form of cultivation of moral feeling is discovered through Kantian critique. Moreover, in arguing that taste is a dormant aspect of human nature, Kant implies that he has sufficiently addressed the worry that the necessity of culture for the experience of sublimity would render taste dependent on convention. Whether Kant's defence of culture is convincing, Deleuze's reading suggests that Kant's worry about contingency at the level of culture can be expanded to cover the critical project itself.

Critique's aim from the beginning is to realise the higher forms of the faculties of mind by identifying and ensuring the proper organisation of active faculties necessary for each. What critique seeks to describe are the conditions for harmony to emerge between the faculties, or, the conditions of common sense. But, critique is a process undertaken by Reason itself. How then, can Reason expect its results to stand up to scrutiny when it acts as judge and jury in its own case? In Kant's claim that Reason poses for itself its own ends Deleuze sees the key to understanding the entire critical philosophy. He does not want to describe critique in terms of its adjudicating role. In Deleuze's mind, critique is not there primarily to discipline or correct Reason. The central task of immanent critique is really a self-reflexive examination by Reason of its own ends, which establishes what those ends are, its own limits or powers, and the conditions of its harmonisation with the other faculties. Critique does discipline, but does so by mapping the productive avenues of power.

The general problem is nonetheless how to achieve Reason's self-knowledge. The answer comes in Reason's peculiar condition of granting respect: as Kant writes, 'Reason grants [respect] only to that which has been able to withstand its free and public examination' (CPR A xi). So, Reason's self-knowledge can only be legitimated if that knowledge has been able to pass the test of 'free and public examination'. Critique, it appears, still relies on 'common sense' for legitimating Reason's ends and, ultimately, establishing morality.

Deleuze distances his reading of Kant from the danger of Reason's inner conflict because he does not see critique as primarily a method for assuring the legitimacy of knowledge by suppressing that conflict. He does not see critique's function in terms of the teleological realisation of external ends. What Deleuze emphasises throughout *Kant's Critical Philosophy* – in a way that is almost clinical in its precision and objectivity – are not Reason's dangers (in relation to which one must establish limitations), but the complex interrelation between Reason's ends (in relation to which one must establish the appropriate hierarchy). When Deleuze does talk about Reason's internal conflict, such as in the account of the genesis of aesthetic common sense, it is terms of its positivity, not its danger. This is echoed in his understanding of critique: it is not a corrective to Reason so much as the instrument for the establishment of the system of Culture. If, as Deleuze writes on the very first page of *Kant's Critical Philosophy*, the 'supreme ends of Reason form the system of Culture' (KCP 1), and the ends of Reason 'form an organic and hierarchical system, which is that of the ends of a rational being' (KCP 7), what is implied is that Kant's critical perspective takes as a principle the organisation of the system of Culture according to the ends of Reason. Moreover, as Deleuze writes, the 'illusions of Reason triumph above all, as long as Reason remains in the *state of nature*' (KCP 26–7). Traditionally, the state of nature is associated with a state of war (or, in an extended sense in which it applies to Kant's perception of Africans and Pacific Islanders, in a state without culture, or indeed any overarching authority). Deleuze explains that for Kant 'Critique is precisely the establishment of this civil state: like the jurist's contract, it implies a renunciation of Reason from the speculative point of view' (KCP 27). This is structurally analogous to the classic example of the formation of a social contract: subjects must give up the freedom to do whatever they can do in exchange for protection of their life and property. In the context of Kant's critical philosophy, subjects must give up their 'freedom' to speculate about noumena in exchange for culture and morality. Thus, two different routes reach the same conclusion: it is Kantian critique that ultimately establishes culture and morality.

For Kant, culture is a necessary formative influence pushing humans toward the perfection of their moral capacities. As a merely instrumental good, Kant values culture only in so far as it contributes to the formation of rational moral men. Thus, only certain kinds of culture – those that 'prepare [men] for a sovereignty in which Reason alone is to dominate' – are valuable (CJ §83). While Kant may believe that he has responded to his worry that culture is a matter of convention, what counts as culture (and therefore what counts as proper cultivation) is determined by the original decision as to what counts as an end of Reason. Critique establishes what counts as an end of Reason and therefore also what counts as proper culture. This original decision is made through an appeal to the test of public examination, that is, to the dogmatic Image of thought. However, Deleuze's reading suggests that what Kant presents as the true interests of Reason are in reality Kant's own interests – or more precisely those interests particular to Kant's social and historical epoch that his work represents through its subjective presuppositions. These hidden, contingent interests that determine culture, Deleuze suggests, are ultimately moral interests.[3]

If Deleuze is right that Kant's critique assumes a particular list and hierarchy of Reason's ends based on hidden moral interests, then there are at least three consequences. First, Kant's moral teleology would become groundless. If morality is assumed to be the destiny of man from the outset, then claiming that morality must be conceived as the highest end of Reason is less convincing. Second, Kant's conception of culture would be understood as a foundational anthropology that raises the empirical to the level of the transcendental. As we have just seen, the only forms of culture valued by Kant are those that prepare men 'for a sovereignty in which Reason alone is to dominate' (CJ §83). What this means is that not all cultures are created equal. Certain cultures are more capable of producing rational moral men than others, and some, problematically, are incapable of forming them at all. But if Kant's conception of the proper culture for moral progress depends on the presupposition of a teleology in which rationality and morality are virtually co-extensive, then his choice of proper culture is developed at the empirical level rather than the transcendental. Third, as we have also seen, for Kant the way in which rational moral men are produced is necessarily through violence. The assumption of the superiority of the moral end of Reason allows Kant to grant legitimacy to the violence of humans' unsocial tendencies because the end of that violence is morality. Likewise, state violence is preliminarily granted legitimacy because it protects social order, another necessary condition for the progress of Reason toward morality from Kant's perspective. Even the violence of war and the imposition of Kant's (white, male, European, tax-paying) models of culture and freedom on subject nations are justified in so far as this is necessary for the creation of a perfectly just and cosmopolitan 'civil constitution' (IUH 'Fifth Thesis').

In summary, Kant's critical philosophy presupposes knowledge about the superiority of the moral end of Reason, but this knowledge is derived from Kant's historical and philosophical milieu. On Deleuze's reading, Kant assumes a moral teleology in order to ground his anthropology and his justification of the necessity of violence for moral and social progress. The practical consequence of this is a philosophical ethos that dramatically limits possibilities of life.

Deleuze's Critical Demoralisation

The problem here, as it has been from the beginning, is that of eradicating subjective presuppositions in the starting point, of cultivating the ability to catch oneself smuggling biased content into the foundational building blocks of one's theory. Thinking through the implicit biases people bring to their way of experiencing and interpreting the world has become more urgent recently as these biases are blamed for the continuation of institutionalised racism, sexism, ableism and many other forms of oppression, for the police brutality experienced disproportionately by people of colour, and for the failure of people in positions of privilege to adequately self-assess that privilege. This is an issue for individuals who do not perceive the racism or sexism hidden within their ways of perceiving and interpreting the world, but it is also important for groups who are aware of the systemic violence against minorities and genuinely desire to be part of the eradication of that violence. Implicit biases are a particular problem for this group because of the frequency with which their best intentions end up reproducing the racism, sexism and other forms of oppression that they wish to resist. For example, the focus in traditional feminism on expanding women's role outside of homemaking, on establishing their reproductive rights and liberating their sexuality, while important goals for white, middle-class, educated women, also implicitly ignored or de-prioritised issues that were more pressing to women of colour, who had been in the workforce for generations and were on the whole more concerned with economic and educational barriers to equality than with overly restrictive idealisations of their gender. This prioritising of the white, middle-class, Western, educated agenda within feminism happened in many instances without the leaders of the feminist movement realising they were perpetuating injustice in their struggle against injustice. These women did not hunt down their own implicit biases, with some even failing to acknowledge their privileged points of view. This is why the larger feminist movement has now almost unanimously accepted Kimberlé Crenshaw's 1991 'intersectional' critique of traditional feminism, which unambiguously pointed out the implicit biases within feminism.[4] Feminists, like most social activists, want their work to have the maximum impact for social justice. Since sincere and thoughtful people have implicit biases that limit the power of their theories, it is imperative to ask whether Deleuze's ethical framework smuggles in implicit biases as well. This is especially pressing given the dawning appreciation within the scholarship of the parallels between Deleuze's theoretical perspective and Kant's. If Kant's critique smuggled in his own implicit biases through its establishment of the proper ends of Reason and the means of cultivating sensibility, does Deleuze's critique do the same? Is there a parallel between Kant and Deleuze at the level of hidden moral interests?

For Kant, the question of 'culture' was how to get the most out of humans by developing sensibility and interpretation through education and training. Similarly for Deleuze, in *Difference and Repetition*, culture is understood as *paideia*, that is, as the general process of acclimatisation to a society's highest ideals that itself represents those ideals as a full and cohesive system. *Paideia* is precisely what Kant means by culture as well. While it is true that for Deleuze the adventure of thought is involuntary, this does not mean that one would not desire it. But it is not something one can will to happen at any moment. All you can do is cultivate in yourself an openness, even a readiness, for thought – and this openness takes the form of training in evaluating presuppositions. This training is what Deleuze understands culture to offer, and it is the principle of the genesis of the experience of the encounter within which thought comes like a 'Eureka!' moment or a sudden revolutionary Idea. But such Ideas only come to those who have cultivated the openness, understanding and ingenuity for them. For Deleuze, culture develops in people the habit (even the need) to dare to think.

If one's level of culture determines the degree to which the encounter may be experienced, the question arises as to what it is that determines the proper culture to be pursued in order to develop this capacity. While Deleuze does not explicitly answer this question in *Difference and Repetition*, the parallels drawn so far between his and Kant's theories of faculties suggest that the answer best suited to Deleuze's work is structurally parallel with Kant's answer: critique. According to Deleuze's reading, for Kant, Reason's ends form Culture and since critique is what determines Reason's ends, critique is also the instrument of the establishment of the system of Culture. Since critique establishes what counts as an end of Reason, it also determines what counts as proper Culture. To what extent does Deleuze's answer to the question of what form of culture should be pursued parallel the one he attributes to Kant? As we have seen, there were three consequences of Deleuze's reading of Kant: the groundlessness of the moral teleology, the diagnosis of a foundational anthropology, and the justification of state violence. Does Deleuze face these consequences as well? Deleuze's critical ethos avoids the most obvious of the criticisms he levels at Kant. Deleuzean critique does not prioritise Reason and does not require a moral teleology. Moreover, in Deleuze, the use of culture built on critique does not hide a foundational anthropology. For Kant, philosophy is the discovery of a priori knowledge. Critique determines the extent to which human Reason is capable of discovering a priori knowledge, and it is the ends of a rational being that organise the entire system of critique – it is these ends that will determine to what extent human reason is capable of attaining a priori knowledge. But for Deleuze philosophy is not the discovery of knowledge – a priori or otherwise. It is the creation of concepts. Philosophy understood as the creation of concepts opens the object of philosophy beyond the discovery of knowledge. Concepts can be created through faculties other than Reason. Philosophy is more than logic. In *What is Philosophy?*, Deleuze and Guattari are careful to distinguish philosophy from reflection, contemplation and communication. Philosophy, they claim, constitutes knowledge through the creation of concepts (WP 5). Doing philosophy involves risking something. It is attempting to capture a moment in thought, much like art 'frames' an affect. This creation of knowledge is thinking. Reason is displaced because the creation of concepts or thinking is so much more than just the logical mastery represented by Reason. Thinking is the mental process associated with knowledge formation; Reason is thinking that has an objective rather than just wandering around. When it is oriented toward an objective, thinking is reasoning. When it is wandering it is thinking. Thinking is wandering whereas Reason is goal-oriented. Crucially, thinking is not therefore necessarily irrational. Thinking expresses a desire, but Reason is a desire, too. It is a desire for mastery. Thinking uses similar tools, but without the desire for domination. Thinking wants to shift what counts as legitimate according to the ideals of immanence, productivity, openness, becoming. Note, however, that there is no hierarchy expressed by the Deleuzian differential theory of faculties.

In Deleuzean critique then, thinking replaces Reason as the faculty that organises the critical project. It is a non-hierarchical and nomadic self-organisation through dispersal that is not undertaken by a subject but is undergone in the subject as a de-individualisation. In *Anti-Oedipus*, Klossowski's commentary on Nietzsche's 'lofty thought' of *Stimmung* is invoked to explain the centrality of thinking to a sort of disharmonious unity or 'tuning' of the soul created through the affirmation of the necessity of the chance series of individualities from which the present ones spring:

> The centrifugal forces do not flee the center forever, but approach it once again, only to retreat from it yet again: such is the nature of the violent oscillations that overwhelm an individual so long as he seeks only his own center and is incapable of seeing the circle of which he himself is a part; for if these oscillations overwhelm him, it is because each one of them corresponds to an individual other than the one he believes himself to be, from the point of view of the unlocatable center. As a result, an identity is essentially fortuitous, and a series of individualities must be undergone by each of these oscillations, so that as a consequence the fortuitousness

of this or that particular individuality will render all of them necessary. (AO 21)

If critique is not a question of discovering the extent to which Reason is capable of a priori knowledge but a question of inventing the mechanisms – the *how* – by which thinking is capable of creating concepts, then, when thinking replaces Reason, the ends of a rational being that organised critique for Kant become for Deleuze and Guattari the production of a nomadic being/assemblage. As Kristensen has argued,

> For Deleuze, philosophy should not aim for truth by representing or discovering a hidden world. It should rather denaturalise the general imperatives for how we represent and understand the given in order to make room to raise problems in new, positive ways. Truth lies in the effort of creating new forms of problems rather than finding the first principle.[5]

Thinking replaces Reason, but thinking must have desire put into it. What do these ends of a nomadic assemblage imply? For Kant, the ends of a rational being are the higher form of the faculties (in the first sense) when they become autonomous and legislative: they are expressed in the speculative, practical, aesthetic and teleological interests of Reason. The ends of a desiring-machine/nomadic assemblage, on the other hand, express the higher form of desires when these become autonomous and legislative: when their productions are connective, inclusive and intensifying (rather than restrictive, exclusive and foreclosing). Desire must be expression rather than repressive. And these ends do not create a system in the way that Kant believed the ends of Reason do. The ends of a nomadic assemblage exceed systems, pointing to a way out.

As noted above, Deleuzean critique also does not require a moral teleology. The ends of a nomadic assemblage are neither moral nor teleological. In fact, Deleuze's practice of critique is specifically aimed at contesting moral teleology and evaluating the subjective presuppositions that keep empirical moral intuitions hidden and implicit. In *Dialogues* Deleuze says, 'There is not a point from where we leave nor a point where we arrive nor where we should arrive' (D 8).[6] As Eugene Holland has argued, Deleuze offers a thought that is utopian, but non-teleological. It is demoralising but also de-territorialising and de-individuating. In chapters 4 and 5 of *A Thousand Plateaus*, territories are sets of environmentally embedded triggers of the self-organising processes of de- and re-territorialisation. Deterritorialisation is the process by which habits are broken. Later, in chapter 11 of *A*

Thousand Plateaus, the notion of the 'refrain' is offered as a means of escaping from territories and forming new ones, or perhaps even existing in a continual process of deterritorialisation or 'consistency' that expresses the critical ethos as a new habit of contesting habits. The habit of creating habits becomes the habit of creating, breaking and then creating new habits.[7] This is the permanent revolution of habit formation that Deleuze sought in the thought without Image.

Whereas in Kant the ends of Reason express Kant's own moral interests, the interests revealed in Deleuze's ends of a nomadic assemblage have been described as primarily negative. But they also have a positive side associated with normativity and the invention of norms. If normativity is traditionally understood to be structured around a number of principles drawn from a sense of the Good or a foundational anthropology, the implication is that ethical law is produced through submission to a central, pre-defined and governing power. This central power then polices the borders 'of what counts as respectable, acceptable and workable as a set of operative norms and values both in society and in scientific, philosophical and cultural practice'.[8] This traditional view of normativity is fundamentally at odds with Deleuze's 'differential notion of normativity'.[9] Since the subject for Deleuze is not a unified, individualistic and autonomous self-correcting agent, the appeal to normativity based on universal principles is irrelevant. Nomadic normativity, while not relativistic in Taylor's sense, is creative, process-oriented and critical of despotism and negativity. While it is sometimes argued that Deleuze is the 'anti-normative thinker par excellence',[10] the emphasis on creation indicates a strong normative orientation in Deleuze's thought. The normativity at issue in Deleuze is evaluative and selective, but without a transcendent, unchanging, dogmatic goal. The normative ideal is one of a progress toward openness that can, however, never be complete because it is always practised alongside the habit of creating habits, of a reterritorialising that is not just expressed in humans. Nietzsche claims that the culture of contradiction, or evaluation, is the biggest step in freeing thought from dogma. This once again resonates with Kant's *Sapere aude* or 'dare to know'. Kant's formula valorises the courage to think for oneself that one only develops with humanistic education and in a society that permits religious and scholarly freedom. Deleuze is making the same move as Nietzsche and Kant, but with his own conceptual personae. For Deleuze, as we have seen, culture is a violent training in evaluating presuppositions, and this means becoming, in the first instance, a

'Russian idiot' (DR 130). The normativity expressed in Deleuze's mature thought does not come from Kantian a priori concepts of universality and necessity in the pure form of law-giving. This would have to come from outside experience. As Kristensen puts it:

> For Deleuze, normativity is concerned with the determination of the critical ('the very principles of what we do'). We should therefore understand critique in a twofold way: a literary sense as criticism and in a philosophical sense, that is, critique as the determination of the transcendental elements (determinable forms, problems and modes of individuation) that constitute 'the conditions of real experience' ... Critique is a necessary element in thinking and critique does not constitute being as such but the ethical principle on which being is given as object. In this sense, it establishes and conditions the synthetic relation between objects of thinking and ethical principles ... This synthetic relation is not the given de facto but is that by which the given is given ... The synthetic relation is not 'a sensible being but the being of the sensible' ... In other words, the synthetic relation is the transcendental, which for Deleuze is that by which something is given.[11]

The norm expressed here is not life, but '*a* life' – what Colebrook calls 'a spark'.[12] The set of ideals it establishes are the actualisations of virtual modes of becoming: 'immanence, rather than the transcendence of universal norms; differential social assemblages, instead of either the assurance of dogma or the cynicism of doxa and the emphasis on the genesis of emerging, transversal collective affirmative values, rather than the implementation of canonical laws'.[13] So the problem is not with ideals, ends or norms, but with negative ones and with the assumption that they are True. If there is no given, normativity has to be invented. The worry is, of course, that without a bedrock structure or power with which to anchor ethical life the result will be moral chaos and relativism. However, the under-narration of the stories of others is intentional. It takes courage to give thinkers the tools to write their own stories.

Finally, culture in Deleuze does not require a foundational anthropology. This is the most difficult problem. Critique determines the system of culture by reference to the ends of a nomadic assemblage. While Deleuze does not assume a moral teleology in so far as his practice of critique is specifically aimed at contesting moral teleology and evaluating the subjective presuppositions that keep our empirical moral intuitions hidden and implicit, there are still two concerns. First, whether the use of culture in Deleuze's differential theory of faculties implies an appraisal in which certain cultures are more valuable than others, thus undercutting the power of critique as a transcendental 'handbook'. Second, whether the violence at the heart of culture (and at the heart of Deleuze's notions of the Idea and the encounter) undercuts the liberationist ideal of critique as a 'way out'.

Firstly, as we have seen, while the accounts of culture in *Difference and Repetition* and *Kant's Critical Philosophy* agree about its definition and place, there is an important difference as well. In the Kant book, Deleuze emphasises how culture prepares humans for the feeling of the sublime, which in turn prepares them for the moral law. It is the faculty of taste, properly cultivated, which allows one to experience in the sublimity of Nature a symbol of the suprasensible. Since the faculty of taste was always latent within humans and only needed to be drawn out by proper cultivation, what this capacity to feel the suprasensible symbolised in Nature shows is that it is human destiny to develop morality. In *Difference and Repetition*, on the other hand, the system of Culture is determined by thought's highest form, which is in turn determined by critique. Since critique is immanent, it is not determined by any particular goal or destiny beyond Deleuze's self-acknowledged definition of philosophy as 'breaking with *doxa*' – in other words, finding a 'way out' by creating something new.

Secondly, it is important to distinguish the two senses of culture in *Difference and Repetition*: culture as *paideia* and culture as 'culture of the times' (DR 158). The latter is the 'grotesque image of culture' that calls upon people 'to choose according to his or her taste, on condition that this taste coincides with that of everyone else' (DR 158). This grotesque image of culture encourages a sort of judgement of taste that seems singular but only counts as taste if it agrees with everyone else. It represents the pedagogical method of common sense. The second sense of culture is *paideia* (DR 165). *Paideia* is a transliteration of the ancient Greek παιδεία, which means 'child-rearing', 'training' or simply 'education'. The Oxford English Dictionary defines *paideia* as:

> Education, upbringing; *spec.* an Athenian system of instruction designed to give pupils a rounded cultural education, esp. with a view to public life. Hence: the sum of physical and intellectual achievement to which an individual or (collectively) a society can aspire; a society's culture.

This definition, however, is at odds with Deleuze's contrast of culture as *paideia* with methods dictated by common sense. It is fair to ask in what sense *paideia*'s education in society's highest ideals is different from method's determination of thought through the presupposition of common sense. Both appear to be governed by empirical presuppositions. Moreover, Deleuze's suggestion of culture's superiority over method might seem to imply an elitism privileging whatever culture Deleuze deems the proper one. Yet, when Deleuze is talking about culture, he does not mean a particular society's culture, as he is clear that this sense of culture is reserved for the 'grotesque' image (DR 158). Rather, Deleuze means a philosophical culture whose ideal is a constant questioning, problematising and creating. The contrast between culture and method is thus less about the existence of presuppositions and more about the contingency, comprehensiveness and involuntariness of culture and its value as a model for Deleuze's conception of learning as the movement from the empirical to the transcendental forms of the faculties. Indeed, by aligning the movement of learning with that of culture, Deleuze is actually drawing attention to his own presuppositions – that is, to his ideal of philosophy as the evaluation of presuppositions. This ideal is not an empirical presupposition taken as an in-principle feature of human nature, but a starting point for philosophy that acknowledges the necessity of evaluating every starting point – indeed, that makes that evaluation the fundamental condition of philosophising.

As such, the *paideia* necessary as a preparatory education is the critique itself – the critique of the powers and limits of the faculties that opens the analysis of time and ends with the adventure of the fractured I. For Deleuze the system of culture is determined by thought's highest power – that is, by the ideal of a thought without Image – and the highest power of thought is determined by critique, since critique is what identifies, evaluates and determines the means of realising the highest intrinsic power of each of the faculties. In contrast with Kant, Deleuze's determination of culture does not presuppose empirical 'knowledge' or moral interests. Deleuze's immanent critique does not presuppose any particular goal he may have wanted to impute to it beyond his self-acknowledged definition of philosophy as 'breaking with *doxa*' (DR 134). If culture is determined through immanent critique's examination of the faculties' intrinsic power, without either hierarchising the faculties or imposing on them a certain ideal organisation based on 'rational' constraints, Deleuze is not making an implicit appraisal in which certain cultures are more valuable than others. Deleuze's system of culture requires the development of a critical ethos that persistently seeks a 'way out' by evaluating presuppositions and creating new Ideas, new thoughts without Image, out of the openness and wonder one develops toward experience through one's evaluation of one's own presuppositions – that is, of one's own society, knowledge and moral values. Thus, since the critical ethos expressing Deleuze's ontology is built on the constantly renewed evaluation of all presuppositions, it does not limit possibilities of life but arouses life to expand to the very limits of its power. To disentangle the philosophical concept of becoming from any teleology is to rethink becoming as a kind of Nietzschean transvaluation in which minoritarian subjects can no longer be defined simply by their exclusion from dominant social categories but must become-minoritarian in order to deterritorialise themselves from the dominant modes of hierarchy and create their own affirmative values. Culture as *paideia* does not seem to imply any particular culture in much the same way as becoming-woman or becoming-minor do not imply specific women or minorities. This is not identity politics but a flight from all molar identifications. However, the problem of subjective presuppositions may merely go underground. Does it persist at the level of educational practices? Is the critical ethos cultivating a people exclusionary in so far it is based on a common education? What would a schizoanalytic educational practice look like? Does it have to be violent?

Notes

1. Immanuel Kant, 'An Answer to the Question: What is Enlightenment?', in *Practical Philosophy*, ed. and trans. Mary Gregor, Cambridge: Cambridge University Press, 1996.
2. But any such constitution must necessarily be cosmopolitan. In other words, it must not be restricted to any one country and its inhabitants, but belong to the world at large. Thus, there is a larger purpose of Nature at play here. The violence and devastation of war are Nature's means to teach the human species that they must 'institute a cosmopolitan condition to secure the external safety of each state' (IUH 'Seventh Thesis').
3. This has repercussions throughout the critical project. As the French philosopher and historian Michel Souriau claims in his *Le Jugement réfléchissant dans la philosophie critique de Kant* (Paris: Alcan, 1929), a book Deleuze would have been familiar with even though he does not cite it directly, the idea of reflective judgement (which includes the judgments of taste and teleological judgments at issue here) connects all the critiques even though Kant does not introduce it until the *Critique of*

Judgement. This adds credence to Deleuze's idea that Kant's teleology can be seen as the central idea on which the critical project stands.
4. Kimberlé Crenshaw, 'Mapping the Margins: Intersectionality, Identity Politics, and Violence Against Women of Color', *Stanford Law Review* 43:6 (1991), pp. 1241–99.
5. Kristensen, 'Thinking Normativity in Deleuze's Philosophy', pp. 17–18.
6. See also TP 36, 468.
7. This is connected with chapter 12 of *A Thousand Plateaus* in which the war machine is described as a form of social organisation that fosters creativity by 'reterritorializing on deterritorialization itself'.
8. Braidotti and Pisters, 'Introduction', in *Revisiting Normativity with Deleuze*, p. 1.
9. Ibid.
10. Claire Colebrook, 'Norm Wars', in Braidotti and Pisters (eds), *Revisiting Normativity with Deleuze*, p. 81.
11. Kristensen, 'Thinking Normativity in Deleuze's Philosophy', p. 13.
12. Colebrook, 'Norm Wars', p. 83.
13. Braidotti and Pisters, 'Introduction', p. 2.

6

Violence of Critique

The problem of violence is endemic in philosophical thinking. The desire for mastery, rational proof, persuasive means and certainty are hallmarks especially of modern and contemporary Western philosophy. In 'How is this Paper Philosophy?', Kristie Dotson discusses the implications of what she calls 'the culture of justification' model of philosophy. This model alienates many philosophers from non-white and non-Western backgrounds due to disciplinary pressures in which their ideas and practices are evaluated in relation to 'presumed commonly-held univocally relevant justifying norms'.[1] But philosophy can be richer than this. As Robert C. Solomon has put it, the failure of 'thin' contemporary philosophy to take seriously and seek out multiple, broad forms of practice 'bespeaks a profound impoverishment'.[2] Enriching philosophy through inclusiveness and the self-critique of its own presuppositions is imperative if it is to continue to be of value to ethical thinking and practices. This imperative is particularly relevant due to the problems of violence experienced today, from the micro-violences well-meaning people commit despite their best intentions to the fascist forms of violence that have made refugees of millions. Taking a deeper look at whether the Deleuzian ethos of critique is guilty of this in the articulation of specific educational practices is thus the next step.

Fascist Anti-fascism

For the purpose of developing the critical ethos, it is helpful to borrow some of the vocabulary from Walter Benjamin's 1921 essay 'On the Critique of Violence'. Here Benjamin explores the implications of violent interventions on behalf of the state by those empowered to exercise a law-preserving function. In relation to the Deleuzian ethos and educational practices, this is the problem of fascist anti-fascism that acts as a form of thought policing. This anxiety about police violence resonates deeply today in the wake of the militarisation of local police forces along with their seeming immunity to accountability. Benjamin, for his part, distinguishes 'law-preserving' or police violence from 'law-making' or terrorist violence. 'Law-making' violence is required to found a state – but once the state is established, its terrorist 'law-making' violence is legitimised, thereby becoming 'law-preserving' police violence. 'Law-preserving' police violence is thus the new name for terrorist 'law-making' violence after it has become legitimised by the state it served to found.[3] As Benjamin analyses it, violence is considered legitimate when its end is justified. Of course, the context for legitimacy is defined by the state, or, more broadly, the system of values with majority power – though not necessarily majority numbers. The problem is not just that this leaves society with few resources for questioning state-sponsored violence, but that the system of values responsible for granting legitimacy (of violence as well as everything else) resists internal change by suppressing difference and minority values and rewarding an ethic that refuses to question the basic presuppositions of its context. This is police violence on the level of thought. The difference between 'police violence' and 'police violence on the level of thought' is that the latter is sanctioned not by the state but by the system of values with majority power. To make a clear distinction between the two, the term 'police violence' will be reserved for state-sanctioned violence and the term 'value-sanctioned violence' reserved for violence at the level of thought.

Benjamin goes on to pose the question of whether violence could ever be justified as a 'pure means' in itself, independent of whether it is applied to just or unjust ends. Is there a way to evaluate violence in itself regardless of what ends it might be used to accomplish? Benjamin's point is that any attempt to evaluate violence on the basis of whether it is a means to just or unjust ends is doomed to fail because such an evaluation could only ever give criteria for the cases of the use of violence, not criteria for the use of violence itself. Unfortunately, after raising this possibility of violence conceived as 'pure means', Benjamin abandons it. It is important to keep in mind that thinking of violence as 'pure means' means thinking of violence that does not have an end. The rest of Benjamin's essay focuses on types of violence that refer to very specific ends – in particular, the end of the end of history itself.[4] One thinker of this type of end was Immanuel Kant.

As described in more detail in the previous chapter, 'unsocial sociability' is Kant's term for the tension between human beings' natural inclination to associate with others and their natural resistance to living socially. For Kant, nature has ordained that humans' violently unsocial sociability operates as the force behind the progress of their Reason. The end of Reason explains and justifies the means of violence. However, this violence must be curtailed in society in order to provide the stability for progress. Thus, the state is sanctioned in its use of violence against the violence of individuals where the latter poses a threat to social cohesion. But what is most important for Kant is that the self-regulation of one's unsocial tendency is equivalent with morality. Morality is self-legislation, that is, autonomy. Morality is the highest level of insight it is possible to cultivate in Reason, thus morality is the highest end of Reason and of Nature. Morality is thus also the value responsible for granting legitimacy. Morality grants legitimacy to the violence of humans' unsocial tendencies because the end of that violence is morality itself. Likewise, state-sanctioned violence is granted legitimacy because it protects social order, a necessary condition for the progress of Reason toward morality. Of course, when Kant presents morality as the ultimate value responsible for granting legitimacy, he takes the responsibility for granting legitimacy away from the state. If, for example, the state were to violently suppress diversity of religious belief, human beings' freedom to use their own reason would thereby also be suppressed. But since for Kant the freedom to use one's own reason is the single most important factor in Reason's moral progress, any violence against that freedom would be unjust, even if it were sanctioned by the state. So, while Kant has not given an account of violence as a 'pure means', he has offered resources for evaluating the legitimacy of state-sanctioned violence. However, the problem with Kant's solution – at least the one focused on here – is that he has not provided resources for addressing the deeper problem of value-sanctioned violence.

Value-sanctioned violence is deeper than state-sanctioned violence because it is hidden in presuppositions that are much more difficult to evaluate. Evaluating one's government according to an external standard is much easier than evaluating one's own evaluational context itself. But it is just such an evaluation of values that a Deleuzian ethos of critique is capable of offering. In *Difference and Repetition*, Deleuze claims to see in Kant's idea of critique the power to evaluate everything. And so he laments that Kant's unwillingness to put Reason's ends of knowledge, morality and faith into question hobbled the critical exercise and led to Kant's failure to evaluate his own evaluational context. When in *Kant's Critical Philosophy* Deleuze tries to reconstruct Kant's entire critical project from the point of view of Reason's relationship to its own ends, he does so in order to identify the precise point at which the Kantian critique failed – so that he can develop a more radical critique that will succeed.

Deleuze begins *Kant's Critical Philosophy* with the claim that the primary function of Kantian critique is to determine both 'the true nature of reason's ... ends' and 'the means of realizing these [ends]' (KCP 3). Deleuze identifies the true nature of Reason's ends by describing the first of the two senses he attributes to the word 'faculty'. The first sense refers to the 'faculties of mind': knowledge, desire and the feeling of pleasure and pain. The faculties of mind are capable of both a higher and a lower form. In their lower form, they exhibit a relationship of dependency; in their higher form, they become autonomous. Each faculty of mind's higher form corresponds to an end of Reason. When the faculty of knowledge achieves its higher form, it expresses the speculative end of Reason, which is to legislate over phenomena. When the faculty of desire achieves its higher form, it expresses the practical end of Reason, which is to realise moral good in the world. And when the faculty of the feeling of pleasure and pain achieves its higher form, it corresponds to the teleological end of Reason, which is to discover purpose in the agreement of Nature with the faculties (KCP 54). These three ends correspond to the three questions Kant poses to 'answer all the interests of my reason' in the 'Canon of Pure Reason': 'What can I know?', 'What ought I to do?' and 'What may I hope?' (CPR A805/B833). The higher, autonomous, forms of the faculties of mind are thus the true nature of Reason's ends.

Once that true nature has been identified, Kantian critique still has the problem of discovering the means of realising these ends. The question is how each faculty of mind becomes autonomous or 'finds *in itself* the law of its own exercise' (KCP 4). This is where Deleuze introduces the second sense of the word 'faculty'. The 'active faculties' are imagination, understanding and Reason (KCP 9). They are the sources (respectively) of reproductions, concepts and Ideas. An end of Reason can only be achieved when the active faculties organise their interactions according to the ideal of 'common sense'.[5] As Kant describes it, common sense is an ideal of comparative rational evaluation operating at the a priori level.[6] On Deleuze's reading, common sense is the condition of harmony between the active faculties in so far as it makes communication between them possible by posing the ideal of a particular mode of representation gleaned from a hypothesised form of collective human Reason. Common sense thus provides a standard for the harmonious proportion of the faculties issued as an a priori rule of representation itself. There may be innumerable ways of representing and therefore thinking, but diverging too much from the way set by common sense leads to nonsense. What counts as 'common sense' is any a priori expression of a system of values with majority power. As a presupposition at the level of what counts as Reasonable activity, this amounts to a form of value-sanctioned violence against thought.

This value-sanctioned violence is necessary because while the active faculties do have a natural tendency to align with common sense, they have an equally natural tendency to resist common sense by tending toward internal illusions and illegitimate exercises.[7] The main problem comes from Reason itself. As the source of Ideas that exceed the possibility of experience, Reason offers 'the illusion of a positive domain to conquer outside experience', thus encouraging the other faculties to neglect their common-sense sanctioned legitimate employment (KCP 25). Of course, as Deleuze points out, if Reason were merely speculative it is unlikely it would ever attempt to know things in themselves (KCP 6). If it is supposed, however, that Reason's ends form a hierarchy and that the moral end is superior to the speculative one, then Reason's interest in things in themselves begins to appear 'legitimate and natural' (KCP 27). The moral end is superior to the speculative because morality is *meant* to be realised (KCP 39). Reason is *meant* to progress toward morality. The problem is that the realisation within the sensible world of something as suprasensible as morality requires an accord between sensible and suprasensible Nature.

The teleological end of Reason is the discovery of that accord. This end is realised when the faculty of the feeling of pleasure and pain achieves its higher form, for which a certain organisation of active faculties is necessary – an organisation one would expect to be determined by aesthetic common sense. Unlike speculative and moral common sense, however, aesthetic common sense cannot simply be assumed. The organisation of aesthetic common sense must be produced spontaneously among the active faculties as an exercise of their freedom. Thus Kant provides an account of the genesis of aesthetic common sense through a critique of the experience of the sublime. As we have seen, the experience of the sublime forces humans to measure themselves against the apparent omnipotence of Nature, allowing them to discover in their own faculty of Reason a superiority over Nature. Humanity's powerlessness in the face of the sublime paradoxically reveals Reason's power to rise above inclination, above Nature, for the sake of rational beings' highest principles. Humans are capable of morality, not just instinct. Thus it is from within this genesis that humans discover their destiny as moral beings. This is why Kant insists that the pre-eminence of Reason is only rendered intuitable through the inadequacy of the imagination (CJ §23). As Deleuze puts it: 'the sense of the sublime is engendered within us in such a way that it prepares a higher finality and prepares us ourselves for the advent of the moral law' (KCP 52).

There is a danger that Deleuze's own theory of culture ties him to the same problems of racial, ethnic, gender and class bias that feminists and other theorists sensitive to the implicit presuppositions that skew 'objective' ontological stories have identified in Kant. Deleuze utilises the same logic of power in the movement of faculties, the same emphasis on the importance of a preparatory education of the senses for an ethical life, and the same language of violence in the progress of thinking. The question is whether these overlaps constitute a failure at the heart of the critical ethos.

In Kant, the experience of the sublime forces the imagination to confront its powerlessness in the face of an Idea of Reason. That powerlessness must then be internalised in relation to Reason as it operates through humanity to achieve species-level moral progress. In Deleuze, the story is uncannily similar. Thought achieves its higher form when forced by the experience of the encounter to confront its limits in terms of both that which it is incapable of thinking and that which it can only think. This confrontation with powerlessness is 'the greatest power' in so far as it reveals the soul or dark precursor as the hidden manifestation of Difference itself as the being of becoming. The 'power' of the subject – its activity – comes from the affirmation of this constant, unending and all-encompassing becoming. This is not a valorisation of the individual's rise above illusion but an unlocking of the power to transform and de-individuate, moving toward a thorough life-synthesis.

The language of violence is as much a feature of Deleuze's work as of Kant's. The justification – even necessity – of violence for the progress of thinking is the same in both. This is concerning from within Deleuze's perspective because violence is so often employed to impose ways of thinking and acting that are met with resistance – precisely what Deleuze is keen to avoid. Violence is more often a force for oppression, coercion and bullying than it is for freedom and dogged self-evaluation. In *Difference and Repetition*, real thought is generated from a violent training or culture in so far as such a culture is the genetic principle of the experience of encounter. Despite the changes Deleuze's immanent version of critique makes to the practical implications of the theory of faculties, he acknowledges that his account does not make history any less bloody:

> History progresses not by negation and the negation of negation, but by deciding problems and affirming differences. It is no less bloody and cruel as a result. Only the shadows of history live by negation: the good enter into it with all the power of a posited differential or a difference affirmed; they repel shadows into the shadows and deny only as the consequence of a primary positivity and affirmation. For them, as Nietzsche says, affirmation is primary; it affirms difference, while the negative is only a consequence or a reflection in which affirmation is doubled. That is why real revolutions have the atmosphere of fetes. (DR 268)

When Deleuze refers to 'negation' and 'the negative' here he is referring to one of the many facets of the dogmatic Image of thought. The main idea is that even when changes to ones practices have been made, when the critical ethos is lived by identifying, evaluating and affirming limits, and when a thought without Image has been created, it does not make history any the less violent.

Deleuze's description of the genesis of aesthetic common sense marks a shift in the way he reads Kant's conception of critique. When critique is first introduced, its function is defined as that of identifying and realising Reason's ends. By the time critique is applied to the teleological end of Reason, its function has become that of identifying and realising the powers inherent to Reason as well as imagination. Critique identifies the faculties' limits, but these limits must be understood not as weaknesses but as 'the extremity of [their] power'. As we have seen, this also marks a shift in the way Deleuze reads limitation, which is no longer thought of in terms of merely imposing a maximum by which to rein in Reason's ambition, but in terms of identifying the full extent of a faculty's intrinsic power. Each faculty's limit defines its power. Critique will therefore condemn not the faculties' attempts to exceed their limits but their failures to reach those limits. Moreover, since it is violence that makes the faculties' limits discernible, this subtly non-teleological critique gives us resources with which to undermine the legitimisation of violence conceived as a means of imposing on thought and action an end that is merely presupposed as legitimate.

Deleuze's reading of critique in *Kant's Critical Philosophy* thus equips Kant with some resources for evaluating both state-sanctioned and value-sanctioned violence. The non-teleological critique evaluates faculties in themselves, in terms of their intrinsic power. In other words, it is an evaluation of faculties as 'pure means', without referring them to ends. Deleuze takes up this non-teleological conception of critique himself in *Difference and Repetition*. There he is emphatic: Kant abandoned the critical exercise just short of putting into question Reason's ends themselves. On one level the problem is Kant's refusal to renounce the presupposition that morality is Reason's highest end. On another, it is his refusal to renounce teleological thinking entirely. But at the deepest level, both Kant's moral and teleological presuppositions belong to the dogmatic Image of thought (DR 131). Deleuze's radical critique of that Image involves a violence against what is presupposed as legitimate, against implicit biases. But this 'violence' is not of the type that denies difference 'so as to conserve or prolong an established historical order'; rather, it 'speaks in the name of a creative power, capable of overturning all orders and representations in order to affirm Difference in the state of permanent revolution which characterises eternal return' (DR 53). Deleuze is looking for no less than a thought without Image that bears within it the resources to resist ever becoming an Image. So, even though this violence is carried out in the name of a thought without Image, since the latter is not a new Image of thought, it does not establish a new value according to which legitimacy can be measured.

When the legitimacy of violence is defined by the state, on what grounds can that violence be evaluated? This question can be asked in more general terms. When legitimacy is defined by any presupposed value, on what grounds can the legitimacy of that value be evaluated? When Nietzsche calls for an 'evaluation of values', it is this level of analysis at which he aims. In attempting to provide a 'critique of violence', Benjamin suggests that rather than thinking of legitimacy as conferred by the 'end' of a state or a value, we instead try to legitimise 'means' in themselves. This is a call to develop an account of 'pure means' independent of presupposed ends as a resource to evaluate the legitimacy of the state and value monopoly on legitimacy. Deleuze offers the resources to conceive of violence as 'pure means' in his account of a thought without Image. A thought without Image resists the politically conservative way of thinking of violence as a means to either legitimate or illegitimate ends in so far as it furnishes the conditions of creative thinking for no end, and even resists the formation of ends by constantly re-evaluating itself. Here the problem of subjective presuppositions and violence is addressed by contesting both state- and value-sanctioned violence if they become law-preserving in a way that does not proceed from the immanent desires and conditions of the real. When that happens the revolutionary becomes reactionary, limiting autonomy and condescendingly imposing its ideals rather than cultivating inclusive, participatory forms of progress. Deleuze and Guattari diagnose this problem in *Anti-Oedipus* when they discuss attempts to discover the Oedipal structure among African and Indian peoples:

> How are we to understand those who claim to have discovered an Indian Oedipus or an African Oedipus? ... The competence, the honesty, and the talent of these authors – psychoanalysts specializing in Africa – are beyond question. But the same applies to them as to certain psychotherapists here: it would seem that they don't know what they are doing. We have psychotherapists who sincerely believe they are engaged in progressive work when they apply new methods for triangulating the child: but watch out – a structural Oedipus, and this time it isn't imaginary! The same is true of the psychoanalysts in Africa who apply the yoke of a structural or 'problematical' Oedipus, in the service of their progressive intentions. There or here, it's the same thing: Oedipus is always colonization pursued by other means, it is the interior colony, and we shall see that even here at home, where we Europeans are concerned, it is our intimate colonial education. (AO 169–70)

Well-meaning psychoanalysts impose the Oedipal structure when they ignore the real conditions of production and desire in Africa and India and proceed to colonise the minds of these peoples with a wholly ill-fitting theory. Filip Stabrowski offers a contemporary example of such an approach in contrasting 'new build' condominiums introduced by realty developers in the traditionally Polish neighbourhood of Greenpoint in Brooklyn with the neighbourhood's own community-driven efforts to improve its livability, sustainability and traditional beauty through renewal and rejuvenation projects.[8] While the real estate development is an example of the violence of gentrification, the community projects are an example of participatory progress rooted in the desires and living conditions of real people and environments. In Benjamin's language, what a Deleuzian ethos offers by way of addressing these concerns is the idea of critique as law-making violence that resists becoming law-preserving violence. Of course, as Deleuze and Guattari make clear, the Oedipal structure imposed on Africans by well-meaning psychoanalysts is also the 'interior colony' of even white, Western thinkers, due to its fulfilling a dogmatic 'law-preserving' function within an 'intimate colonial education' that shuts down our ability to respond flexibly to the real. This, then, suggests the need to take a closer look at the role of education in potentially playing the part of a hidden moral bias.

Violence in Education

Why does Deleuze describe culture as violent? On the one hand, the term 'violence' has a much broader usage in the French language than it does in English. It would be an ordinary thing for a particularly bright and jarring colour to be described as 'violent' in French. On the other hand, Deleuze connects his use of the word 'violence' with the word *cruauté* (cruelty) – which does not have the same broad application as 'violence' in everyday French – when he writes of culture that it is an involuntary adventure which 'links a sensibility, a memory and then a thought, with all the cruelties and violence necessary ... to "provide a training for the mind"' (DR 215). The use of the word 'cruelty' here immediately calls to mind the work of Antonin Artaud, whom Deleuze refers to frequently in the context of the genesis of thought and whose book, *The Theatre and its Double*, famously theorises a surrealist form of theatre called the Theatre of Cruelty (DR 114). There Artaud writes that, 'without an element of cruelty at the root of every spectacle, the theatre is not possible. In our present state of degeneration it is through the skin that metaphysics must be made to re-enter our minds.'[9] In Artaud's usage 'cruelty' does not refer to torture or the sadistic infliction of pain. Rather, it is defined by physical austerity and determination – as if it were an attempt to make scepticism felt. 'Cruelty' in Artaud's sense is the condition of true spectacle in so far as spectators must submit themselves to an attempt at entering a point of view that shatters their everyday reality. With Artaud's perspective as background, Deleuze's use of 'violence' is contextualised within the necessarily vertiginous experience of evaluating one's deepest presuppositions.

In the above-quoted passage, where Deleuze refers to the violence necessary 'to "provide a training for the mind"', he is quoting Nietzsche. In Nietzsche's work violence does not have the same valence as it does for other thinkers. In *The Gay Science*, culture is violent in so far as it is an imposition. We see this clearly in Nietzsche's claim that culture is a compulsory deformation: that 'one is master of one's own trade at the price of also being its victim'.[10]

But what is the goal of this violent training for Deleuze? We can take a clue from Nietzsche when he writes that:

> The ability to contradict, the acquired *good* conscience accompanying hostility towards what is familiar, traditional, hallowed – [this] . . . constitutes what is really great, new, and amazing in our culture; it is the step of all steps of the liberated spirit.[11]

Nietzsche is claiming that a culture of critical evaluation, or 'acquired good conscience' in hostility to sedimented thought, is the background valuation for freeing thought from dogma. It is the ethos that cultivates the soul to dare to chase learning and growing without knowing. This only goes so far for an ethos of learning, however, as Nietzsche's ethics have come under significant attack as elitist, exclusionary and insensitive to vulnerability and care.[12] Another model for the kind of violence necessitated by Deleuze's critical ethos comes from the increasingly popular 'community of philosophical inquiry' school of education. This is a model developed from John Dewey's work by Matthew Lipman as early as the 1970s. As Michael Burroughs and Jana Mohr Lone describe it: 'a community of philosophical inquiry is an educational space that prioritises dialogue and student engagement as catalyzed by the philosophical insights and interests of the participants'.[13] The goal of the programme is not to imprint students with factual knowledge or to discipline docile citizens. It seeks instead to develop the philosophical sensitivity of especially pre- and post-college people by approaching them as equal participants in creating a caring intellectual partnership rooted in philosophical questions immediately relevant to their own lives. This is the same distinction Deleuze draws when he insists that learning ought to be not the art of identically reproducing facts, but a mode of participation, a 'repetition which is no longer that of the Same, but involves the Other – involves difference' (DR 23). It is empowering in so far as learners are encouraged to think of themselves as important contributors to creating understanding, and it is disruptive of the 'thin' contemporary way of practising philosophy limited by 'the culture of justification' in so far as it treats the non-traditional voices of children, minorities and prisoners, not as deficient in reason, but as embodying a different world that enriches thought by contesting the prevailing norms of society. This type of model of education is experienced by both teachers and students as violent and profoundly disruptive to their traditional roles. However, this kind of violence that forces the subject out of the habitual patterns that have limited their potential for growth is crucial. Like the Deleuzian critical ethos, the community of inquiry encourages its own self-critique. Several new works in the field have pointed out the implicit biases toward 'Western', 'heterosexual', 'cisgender' and 'white' perspectives found in the community of inquiry itself. What is interesting about these critiques, however, is that they do not call for a fundamentally different model, but for a transformation of the learner-centric model so as to ensure its greater inclusiveness. This model for participatory, questioning engagement thus encourages the discordant accord at the heart of the genesis of thought.

The question might be asked, however, that if Deleuze's critical ethos is transformative in this sense, then on what basis can one evaluate what one is transforming into? What real costs are justified for the transformation? The Deleuzo-Guattarian theory of subjectivity as nomadic, rhizomatic and largely passive suggests that the notion of humans as self-correcting agents is hyperbolic at best. Humans are more like monkeys riding on the backs of tigers, congratulating themselves on arriving exactly where they always intended. While the Deleuzian ethos embraces freedom, emphasizes a critical and wondering attitude, resists the presuppositions that serve to oppress people, and encourages an attitude of openness, affirmation and celebration for living life to the fullest, these achievements can only be realised by training the unconscious into open-mindedness, inclusivity and constant questioning. The under-narration, the pauses, within the ethics articulated on the basis of Deleuze's relationship to critique may seem like a weakness. But it is not. In fact, the under-narration is its greatest strength. It both offers flexibility in developing moral judgements and emphasises the unavoidable responsibility of defining one's own life. This is a much more difficult prospect than it might seem at face value. For example, the entire contemporary dialogue surrounding who counts as what gender is contingent on illegitimate attempts to extend the reach of one's own narration to others. It is a hard thing to do to let other people define the world for themselves. Likewise, the similar-sounding debate over the cultural appropriation by white people of non-white culture reveals itself to be in fact about how people in positions of privilege block others' self-narrations and empowerment when they colonise their cultural productions without an appreciation of the real, immanent conditions of those productions' genesis. If, as Sholtz has written, 'silence ... provides the essential possibility of communication and community', it is so in the sense that real dialogue and real togetherness requires that thought be allowed to express itself through others' worlds without the imposition of interpretations.[14] How difficult this reorienting has turned out to be for many otherwise liberal-minded people speaks to the prescience of Virginia Held's work as early as the 1970s on cultivating the ideals of mothering as non-judgemental attitudes of care.[15] Genuine care, with the understanding and active practices of support implied within it, is the condition of inclusivity and of a cultural sharing that is not oppressive. But how is cultivating this attitude possible if it is primarily passive and unconscious?

The Desire for Fascism

Deleuze's critical ethos is fundamentally concerned with freedom. One of the problems of describing it in this way is that his theory of culture is ineliminably entwined with the idea of a violent *paideia* or cultural and moral training. But perhaps the current trends in ethics to absolutise tolerance – which seem to be generated from the same insight into fundamental difference that animates Deleuze's ontology – have missed something. Deleuze's aim is not to valorise tolerance as an absolute principle but to point to the violence of learning as a model that forces encounter, creativity and a feedback loop between outer- and inner-generated rules. As Simone Kotva writes:

> Rather than legitimate a regime of classroom flogging or drug-abuse, the violence of Deleuze's universal *paideia* is meted out in small doses, 'little by little . . . itself no small thing', as Zeno, the founder of the Stoic school, is reported to have said. The apprentice paces him- or herself, becomes just 'a little alcoholic, a little crazy, a little suicidal, a little of a guerilla – just enough to extend the crack, but not enough to deepen it irremediably'.[16]

As noted earlier, violence for Deleuze is the necessarily vertiginous experience of contesting one's deepest presuppositions, but it is also something that happens to you without your consent or even your awareness. Much of it is the violence of habituation at the unconscious level; even the resistance to micro-fascism outlined in the ethical imperative to under-narrate is developed primarily through investments in communities of those whose worlds differ from one's own. This transformation is not wilful, but done within and to the subject. The point of this violence understood as an imposed habituation in evaluation is that it constitutes a practical, lived step in breaking with *doxa*. However, although Deleuze's account of the formation of a thought without Image has been presented as a fundamentally passive process, this is not the whole story. Yes, the whole adventure of thought waits on the accident of the encounter, and when the encounter does strike it forces the faculties to their higher forms. From a practical point of view, the necessity of waiting for something that may or may not arrive, combined with the imperative it puts the faculties under when it does arrive, seems to valorise a quietistic attitude. That is, it encourages passivity and non-resistance, as if the encounter's resistance to recognisability were all that were required to really resist the dogmatic Image of thought and its consequence that thought loses its creative freedom and power of change. If this were the case, then whether one effectively resists or not would depend more on luck than work. The problem with this interpretation is that it ignores Deleuze's descriptions of philosophy as the double project of generating 'the act of thinking in thought' (DR 139) and 'breaking with *doxa*' (DR 134). This language, and much more like it throughout *Difference and Repetition*, does not encourage passivity and non-resistance. Doing philosophy must contribute to generating thought and breaking with *doxa*. That is why the models of learning, culture and becoming supplement the differential theory of faculties. Learning operates as a concrete model for the movement from sensibility to thought that emphasises activity. Culture serves as the principle of the genesis of thought without Image in so far as it prepares thinkers for the experience of encounter. Becoming offers a perilous, de-individuating process of growth that is simultaneously deeply personal and aggressively politically deviant.

Subjects will never be rid of the molar – the fascistic – representational thoughts and habits that crystallise into pathology. They can, however, create the space for a culture that resists these pathologies through the construction of and investment in communities of inquiry and contestation that push subjects to limits they may not see themselves as having. If the difficult thing to accept about Deleuze's ethical theory – indeed about many neo-Nietzschean ethical theories – is that he acknowledges and accepts that his account does not make history any less bloody, perhaps the difficulty of ineliminable violence can also be a hidden source of strength. On the other side of living the critical ethos by identifying, evaluating and affirming limits – of creating a thought without Image through the cultivation of a questioning community that encourages the de-individuation and becoming-minor of the subject – perhaps life would be less oppressively violent if the violence of self-critique increased. This is a life that would be freer, more active and more celebratory – for everyone; that would be no longer the protection of bare life but a dare-to-live life. This does not mean that preservation is unimportant – after all, the habituation of breaking habits is its key – but that the immanent conditions of the genesis of creativity, meaning and living should be given the ethical weight they deserve.

Notes

1. Kristie Dotson, 'How is this Paper Philosophy?', *Comparative Philosophy* 3:1 (2013), p. 6.
2. Robert C. Solomon, '"What is Philosophy?" The Status of World Philosophy in the Profession', *Philosophy East and West* 51:1 (2001), p. 101.
3. Walter Benjamin, 'Critique of Violence', *Reflections*, trans. Edmund Jephcott, ed. Peter Demetz, New York: Schocken Books, 1986, pp. 277–300.
4. Ibid. p. 300. Thus the question of the possibility of evaluating violence as 'pure means' is still an open one – and still a pressing one if there continues to be a lack of resources for questioning the legitimacy of state- and value-sanctioned violence.
5. Depending on which of Reason's ends is at stake, the 'common sense' organisation of active faculties necessary to realise it will be different. There is a 'logical common sense' (KCP 66) for the speculative end of Reason, a 'moral common sense' (KCP 23) for the practical end, and an 'aesthetic common sense' for the teleological end.
6. In section 40 of the *Critique of Judgement*, Kant associates the common sense – or as he refers to it, the *sensus communis* – with the 'common understanding of men': 'the Ideal of a sense common to all, i.e. of a faculty of judgement, which in its reflection takes account (*a priori*) of the mode of representation of all other men in thought; in order ... to compare its judgement with the collective reason of humanity'.
7. Just as police violence must subdue unsocial tendencies that threaten to break up the state, the value-sanctioned violence of common sense must subdue the faculties' illusions and illegitimate exercises that threaten nonsense.
8. Filip Stabrowski, 'New Build Gentrification and the Everyday Displacement of Polish Immigrant Tenants in Greenpoint, Brooklyn', *Antipode* 46 (2014), pp. 794–815. See also Arun Saldanha and Jason Michael Adams (eds), *Deleuze and Race*, Edinburgh: Edinburgh University Press, 2013, which uncovers the 'materio-sensorial divergences' involved in race and suggests that Deleuze and Guattari's

immanent analysis is well suited to grasping how bodies are materially differentiated into hierarchies.
9. Antonin Artuad, *The Theatre and its Double*, New York: Grove Press, 1958, p. 99.
10. Friedrich Nietzsche, *The Gay Science*, trans. Josefine Nauckhoff and Adrian Del Caro, ed. Bernard Williams, Cambridge: Cambridge University Press, 2001, §366.
11. Ibid. §297.
12. The project of 'breaking with *doxa*' mirrors Nietzsche's 'evaluation of values', while the project of generating 'the act of thinking in thought' (DR 139) mirrors Nietzsche's 'creation of new values' (DR 136). Deleuze makes the latter connection himself when he writes that '[t]o think is to create – there is no other creation – but to create is first of all to engender "thinking" in thought' (DR 147). There is a deep Nietzscheanism at the heart of Deleuze's way of understanding philosophy that may resist attempts to make it less elitist and individualistic.
13. Jana Mohr Lone and Michael Burroughs, *Philosophy in Education: Questioning and Dialogue in Schools*, London: Rowman and Littlefield, 2016, p. 11.
14. Sholtz, *The Invention of a People*, p. 195.
15. See Virginia Held, *The Ethics of Care: Personal, Political, and Global*, New York: Oxford University Press, 2006; *Feminist Morality: Transforming Culture, Society, and Politics,* Chicago: University of Chicago Press, 1993; 'Feminism and Moral Theory', in *Women and Moral Theory*, ed. Eva Kittay and Diana Meyers, Totowa, NJ: Rowman and Littlefield, 1987; and 'The Equal Obligations of Mothers and Fathers', in *Having Children: Philosophical and Legal Reflections on Parenthood*, ed. O. O'Neill and W. Ruddick, New York: Oxford University Press, 1979.
16. Simone Kotva, 'Gilles Deleuze, Simone Weil, and Stoic Apprenticeship: Education as a Violent Training', *Theory, Culture, and Society* 32:7–8 (2015), p. 109.

Conclusion: Ethics and the Richness of the Possible

By drawing connections between Deleuze's thought and the thought of Immanuel Kant, a space is allowed to emerge for exploring the development of an ethics from Deleuze's immanentist reading of Kantian critique. This space calls for an adjustment in expectations surrounding what counts as ethics. For ethics is not merely the articulation of sets of rules or hierarchies of the good. It is also, and perhaps primarily, an attitude toward life that is habituated and cultivates a character. This character – dramatised by figures such as the Apprentice and the Russian idiot in Deleuze's early work, and expanded to include the nomad, becoming-woman and the minor in his work with Guattari – expresses a way of living Deleuze's ontology of intensive becoming. Moreover, the space created is one that could not be mapped without the comparison to Kant. The deep logic of the faculties that expresses the dynamic of powerlessness becoming power, the transcendental subject for whom a preparatory education of sensibility in culture is tantamount to the formation of a non-fascistic identity, the connection to the long tradition of critical thinking in education as *paideia*, and the platform on which to turn the critique back onto Deleuze, are all features of the ethics mapped out by Deleuze's work that are overlooked when the focus is exclusively on Nietzschean activity/reactivity or Spinozist expressions of worthiness. An understanding of Kant – and especially the idea of critique, the theory of faculties, and the relationship between culture and morality – is crucial for understanding the ethical stakes and promise of Deleuze's philosophy. When this starting point is taken seriously, the critical ethos implicit in much of Deleuze's thought is easy to map, from his earliest works on Nietzsche, Kant and Proust, through the development of the radical critique in *Difference and Repetition*, to its transformation into schizoanalysis in *Capitalism and Schizophrenia*, and finally to its distillation in immanence in his last works. This critical ethos expresses the mode of living an ontology of becoming through a critique of subjectivity and in so doing promotes non-rule-based ethical decision-making as a value-creating and fulfilled way of life.

The four features of Deleuze's debt to Kant – the theory of faculties; the transcendental, multiple subject; the introduction of the passive self; and the idea of culture as *paideia* – all have their corollaries in Deleuze's energetic, materialist ontology of power. And this ontology is itself determined by Deleuze's use of Kantian critique. Critique identifies the faculties' limits, what bodies can do, but these limits must be understood not as weaknesses but as the extremity of their intrinsic power. This critical ethos takes Deleuze's reading of Kant's theory of faculties together with an immanentist reading of critique to form a contemporary picture of the examined life. Its main features include open-mindedness, creativity, community-formation across differences, the self-evaluation of implicit biases, and the realisation of conditions immanent to becoming-other. The reference to Kant reveals another level that requires evaluation: the idea of culture and the moral presuppositions it hides. When the critical ethos is evaluated as a 'handbook' for a 'way out' of dogmatic forms of common sense and their limiting practical consequences, it suggests a way of living characterised by the daily exercise of critical thinking and the permanent de-individuation of ourselves in order to resist fascism as the desire for our own repression within the molar categories of individualism. Thus the real role of immanent critique is to turn the evaluation of presuppositions into a constantly renewed practice of questioning, cultivating an openness to encounters that constitute ruptures with the normalising forces of being. Such forces, Guattari writes, 'blind us to the richness and multivalence of Universes of value which, nevertheless, proliferate under our noses'.[1] Ethics, for Deleuze as for Guattari, is a choice made in favour of this richness of the possible.

Note

1. Félix Guattari, *Chaosmosis: An Ethico-Aesthetic Paradigm*, Bloomington: Indiana University Press, 1995, p. 29.

Index

Antifa, 21n
Apprentice, the, 105–6, 108–14, 118, 150, 153n, 155
Aristotle, 14, 36, 101
Artaud, Antonin, 147
assemblage, 6, 14–15, 54, 77, 83, 131–3
attunement, 92, 94
authenticity, 16, 33–4, 42–4, 47, 96, 106
authoritarianism, 1–4, 6, 8, 16–18
autonomy, 19n, 33, 56, 102–4, 124, 140, 146

Barker, Joe, 16, 23n
Beauvoir, Simone de, 111, 119n
becoming, 6, 14–16, 21n, 22n, 27–9, 34–5, 43–4, 48n, 50, 110–11, 113, 115–17, 119n, 132–3, 136, 143, 151, 155
 animal, 117
 minor, 91, 96, 111, 115
 other, 156
 woman, 96, 110–15, 118n, 155
Bell, Jeff, 6, 19n
Benjamin, Walter, 138–9, 145–6, 152n
Bergson, Henri, 29–30, 79n, 95
Berman, Sheri, 1–2, 17n
Bernasoni, Robert, 50, 77n
Bogue, Ronald, 116, 119n
Braidotti, Rosi, 15, 18n, 20n, 22n, 23n, 33, 46n, 47n, 110–11, 137n
Bryant, Levi, 35–6, 47n, 110, 118n
Buchanan, Ian, 17n, 77n, 97n
Burroughs, Michael, 148, 153n

capacity, 3, 16, 22n, 29, 41, 65, 67, 72, 80, 94, 106, 122, 129, 134; *see also* faculty; power
care, 148, 50
common sense, 28, 34, 36, 38–40, 42, 44–5, 48, 50–1, 53–4, 58–61, 65–7, 70–4, 77, 80–2, 86–90, 93–4, 105–7, 113–15, 120–2, 124–5, 134–5, 141–2, 144, 152, 156
creativity, 9, 13, 29, 45–6, 55, 68, 96, 105, 115–16, 137n, 150, 152, 156
Crenshaw, Kimberlé, 6, 128, 137n
critique, 11, 48n, 49n, 64–5, 102–6, 112–15, 125–6, 133, 138
 Deleuze's immanent/radical, 13–15, 32, 43–6, 51, 77, 80–96, 106–10, 113, 130–1, 133, 144–5, 155–6
 Kantian transcendental, 13–14, 37–8, 43, 46, 52, 80–96, 96n, 97n, 126, 128–9, 142
 of the self, 14–15, 46, 115, 149, 152, 155–6
 see also dramatisation; schizoanalysis
cruelty, 147
culture, 10, 15, 21n, 92–6, 97n, 104, 106–8, 117, 118n, 120–9, 132–6, 138, 143–4, 147, 150–1, 155–6; *see also paideia*

danger, 1, 7, 12, 15–16, 43, 55, 64, 106, 120, 125, 143
dark precursor, 73–5, 143
Debaise, Didier, 44, 49n, 97n
democracy, 1–2, 17n, 19n, 104
Derrida, Jacques, 43
Descartes, Rene, 10, 13, 20n, 40, 60, 84, 113
desire, 14–15, 58, 104, 111, 116, 130–1, 138, 146
 faculty of, 48n, 131, 141
 for fascism, 3–11, 20n, 138, 150–2, 156
 unsocial, 123, 138
deterritorialisation, 15, 65, 77, 105, 111–12, 131–2, 136, 137n
Difference, definition of, 39–40, 55–7, 61

differential theory of faculties, 40, 53–5, 63, 67, 74, 75, 87, 90, 130, 133, 151
discordant accord/harmony, 53, 71–4, 124, 149
dogmatic Image of thought, 11–12, 22n, 35–6, 40, 51–3, 66–7, 76, 80–1, 87, 106–9, 113, 117, 120, 126, 144–5, 151; *see also* moral image of thought
Dotson, Kristie, 138, 152n
doxa (dogma), 41, 50, 55, 58, 70, 81, 85, 94, 105, 107, 110, 112, 133–5, 150–1, 153n; *see also* dogmatic Image of thought
dramatisation, 16, 44–5, 90, 95, 97n, 109–10, 112, 114, 155

Eco, Umberto, 4, 7, 19n
education, 4–6, 15, 76, 93, 95, 101, 104–5, 109–10, 114, 120, 128, 132, 134–6, 138, 143, 146–8, 155
empiricism, 31, 39, 57, 59, 77n, 81–2, 87–8, 96n
encounter, 11, 14–15, 40, 47n, 51, 53, 55–6, 58–63, 68–70, 73, 75–6, 78n, 90–3, 95–6, 105, 107–10, 113, 115–16, 129, 134, 143–4, 150–1, 156
eternal return, 45–6, 145
ethos, definition of, 9, 14, 102–4
Evans, Brad, 3, 8, 14, 18n, 21n
event, 2, 44, 91–3, 95, 98n
experiment, 54, 103
extrinsicism, 59, 80, 86

faculty, 15, 22n, 35–6, 41–2, 47n, 48n, 53, 56–8, 63–78, 90, 105, 108–9, 122–3, 141–2, 144
  of imagination, 41, 55, 90
  of Reason, 13, 41, 55, 64, 84, 89–90, 123, 130
  of sensibility, 40, 58, 61, 86
  of taste, 94, 122, 134
  of thought, 55, 92, 130
  of understanding, 41, 55
  see also capacity; power
fascism, 1–16, 17n, 18n, 19n, 21n, 46, 77, 104, 138, 150, 156
Foucault, Michel, 7, 9, 18n, 21n, 43, 48n, 65, 77, 79n, 91, 102–4, 116–17
  on critique as an ethos, 102–4

fractured-I/self, 32, 42–3, 51, 73–4, 95, 135
freedom, 1, 3, 6, 9–12, 15, 43–4, 46, 57, 61, 64, 68–9, 105–6, 123, 126–7, 132, 140, 142–3, 149–51

genesis, 12–14, 41–3, 53, 59, 65, 68–9, 72–3, 75, 77n, 80, 86–90, 93–5, 109, 120–2, 124–5, 129, 133, 142–4, 147, 149, 151–2
Gibson, Barbara, 115, 119n
Gilson, Erinn, 14, 22n, 47n, 116, 119n
Goulimari, Pelagia, 111, 199n
Guattari, Félix, 1–3, 6–7, 11, 14, 17n, 19n, 20n, 21n, 28–31, 35, 37, 51, 54, 65–6, 77, 82–3, 85, 111–12, 115–16, 130–1, 146, 152n, 155–6

habit, 1, 7–10, 15–16, 29–30, 34–6, 39, 43–6, 47n, 48n, 60, 69, 77, 84, 92, 94–6, 101, 103, 107, 114–15, 117, 129, 131–2, 148, 150–2, 155
Hadot, Pierre, 9, 10–12, 104, 117n
Hare, William, 115, 119n
Heidegger, Martin, 9
Held, Virginia, 15, 153n
hero, 4–5, 7, 9
Higgins, Dick, 91–2
Holland, Eugene, 2, 7, 17n, 82–3, 97n, 131
hooks, bell, 10, 21n
Hughes, Joe, 35, 44–5, 47n, 51, 74, 77n, 85, 97n
Hume, David, 13, 29–31, 35–7, 50, 58, 60, 84, 89, 95

Idea, 15, 44–5, 50, 55, 62–4, 71, 75–6, 90, 92–5, 97n, 108–9, 111–15, 118n, 129, 134–5, 142–3
  moral, 32, 92–4, 121–4
  problematic, 63, 75–6
identity, 4, 6, 8–9, 11–12, 27–9, 32, 36, 38, 40, 42, 130, 155
identity politics, 8, 44, 48n, 111, 113
immanence, 28, 59, 82–4, 87–8, 92, 130, 133, 155
implicit bias, 10–11, 14, 16, 20n, 27, 86, 114, 116–17, 127–8, 143, 145, 149, 156; *see also* subjective presuppositions
individualism, 4–6, 8, 12, 14, 19n, 33, 45, 132, 153n, 156

Index

intensity, 32, 39, 60, 63, 68–9, 73, 78n, 96

Kerslake, Christian, 84, 118n
Klein, Yves, 61, 63, 68–9
  Blue Monochrome, 61, 63, 68–9, 78n
Klossowski, Pierre, 130
Kotva, Simone, 150, 153n
Kristensen, Anders Raastrup, 20n, 36, 109, 131, 133
Kristeva, Julia, 3–4, 9, 18n, 27

limit, 16, 53, 57–8, 63–71, 79n, 81, 83, 88–90, 103, 108, 114, 120, 146, 148, 151, 156
  of faculties, 13–14, 40, 46, 52, 55–8, 62–71, 73, 77n, 84–5, 88, 90, 108–9, 120, 125, 144
  of possibilities of life, 33–4, 43, 127, 136
  see also capacity; power
Lipman, Matthew, 148
logic, 52–3, 69, 81, 89–90, 101, 105, 124, 130, 143, 155
Lone, Jana Mohr, 148, 153n
Lorey, Isabell, 5, 19n
Lorraine, Tamsin, 28–9, 47n

McCoy, Marina Berzins, 116, 119n
machine, 30, 37, 83–4, 112, 137
  desiring-, 54, 69, 85, 131
  war-, 7, 19, 83, 112, 137n
materialism, 82, 86
minor, 50, 91, 96, 111–12, 114–16, 136, 151, 155
  minoritarian, 83, 111, 136
  minority, 5, 11, 21, 111, 128, 136, 139, 148
misogyny, 6, 10, 50
moral image of thought, 80
Mussolini, Benito, 1, 17n, 18n

National Socialism, 4; *see also* Nazism
nationalism, 4–5, 11, 17n, 19n
  ultra-, 1–2, 17n, 18n, 19n
Nazism, 2, 18n, 19n; *see also* National Socialism
Nietzsche, Friedrich, 11, 22n, 47n, 52, 82, 101, 104–5, 107, 112, 132, 144–5, 147–8, 153n
nomad, 23n, 28, 33, 66, 91, 111–12, 130–3, 155
Nozick, Robert, 6, 19n

Oedipus, 6
  Oedipal, 46, 83, 146
O'Neill, Onora, 33–4, 47n, 116
outside, the, 5, 12, 20n, 32, 53, 55, 57, 64, 91, 133–4

paideia (culture), 15, 92–3, 95, 104–5, 107–8, 120, 128–9, 134–6, 150, 155–6; *see also* culture
passive, 29–32, 35, 43–6, 50, 58, 69, 76, 90, 116, 149–51
  self, 45, 80, 95–6, 156
  synthesis, 35–6, 39, 44–5, 50–1, 54, 58–9, 63, 68–9, 74, 76, 85–7, 95
patriarchy, 4, 10–11, 111
Plato, 104
power, 1, 4, 6–8, 12–14, 16, 21n, 28, 35–7, 39–41, 43–6, 48n, 52–77, 81, 83–95, 108–14, 117, 118n, 120, 123–5, 128, 132–6, 139–40, 142–5, 151, 155–6
  love of, 9, 20n, 21n, 104, 123
  powerlessness, 53, 58, 61–2, 69–72, 74–5, 89–90, 95, 107, 116–17, 124, 142–3, 155
  transformative, 12, 143
  see also capacity; faculty
practice, 5, 8–9, 16, 23n, 37, 42, 46, 83, 95–6, 101, 104–5, 107, 109, 111, 114, 123, 132, 136, 138, 144, 150, 156
  critique as, 13–15, 32, 42–6, 49n, 50–1, 63, 76, 81, 84, 87, 90, 95, 105–6, 113, 120, 131, 133, 156
  exclusionary, 1–2, 4–5, 12, 105, 111, 136
  inclusive, 1, 4–5, 9, 131, 138, 150
Protevi, John, 36, 47n
psychoanalysis, 5–6, 69, 83
psychologism, 37–8, 48n, 80–1, 85

racism, 8, 10, 19n, 20n, 116, 127–8
Reich, Wilhelm, 2–4, 6, 17–18n, 19n
Reid, Julian, 3, 8, 14, 18n, 21n
repetition, 5, 27, 37, 47n, 70, 81, 96, 106–9, 114, 148
resistance, 3, 8, 11, 21, 27, 29, 31, 33, 55, 77, 91, 110, 115–16, 143, 150–1
rhizome, 28
Russian idiot, 106–14, 133, 155

schizoanalysis, 14, 48n, 83, 111–12, 155
Semetsky, Inna, 13, 22n
sensation, 39–40, 58–62, 68, 86, 109
sensibility, 39–40, 48n, 54, 55, 58–63, 68–70, 73, 75, 78n, 86–7, 91–2, 95–6, 105, 108, 128, 147, 151, 155
sensitivity, 92–3, 95, 108, 148; *see also* vulnerability
sentiendum, 60, 75
Shestov, Lev, 107
shock, 59–60, 62–3, 74, 90, 109
Sholtz, Janae, 6, 19n, 91–3, 96, 110–12, 115, 149
  on intersectional transversality, 6, 112
singularity, 56–7, 61
Smith, Dan, 16, 36, 58
Solomon, Robert C., 138, 152n
Spinoza, Baruch, 29, 85, 101
spirit, 16, 23n, 72, 101–2, 111, 148
  spiritual, 101–2, 104, 107, 117
Stabrowski, Filip, 146, 152n
subjective presuppositions, 10, 82, 120; *see also* implicit bias
subjectivity, 15, 23n, 27–8, 30, 32–5, 42, 46n, 48n, 95, 98n, 149, 155
sublime, 15, 53, 57–8, 62–3, 65, 71–2, 74, 78–9n, 80, 86–7, 89–95, 120–2, 124, 134, 142–3
synthesis, 31, 35–6, 44–6, 51, 74, 85–6, 96, 143

Taylor, Charles, 5, 9, 19n, 33–4, 42–3, 132
teleology, 97n, 126–7, 129, 131, 133, 136, 137n
  non-teleological, 97n, 106, 108–9, 112, 114, 145
  teleological, 12, 14, 22, 42, 67, 88, 125, 131, 136n, 141–2, 144–5, 152n
totalitarianism, 8, 96
transcendental, 13–15, 31, 35–42, 49n, 52–9, 61, 64, 68–70, 73–6, 77n, 80, 82–5, 87–8, 96n, 113, 127, 133–5, 155–6
Twain, Mark, 32

unsocial sociability/tendency, 122–4, 127, 139–40, 152

violence, 5, 20n, 21n, 45, 59–60, 62, 78n, 89, 91, 105, 123–4, 127–9, 134, 136n, 138–40, 143–8, 150–2
  of encounter, 56, 62, 68–70, 73–6, 90, 108–9
  state-sponsored/police, 20n, 127–8, 139–40, 145, 152n
  value-sanctioned, 127–8, 138–40, 142–6, 152n
Virilio, Paul, 19n, 20n, 112
virtual, 48n, 110, 133
vulnerability, 33–4, 90, 92–3, 95, 112, 116–17, 148; *see also* sensitivity

war-machine, 155, 195
White, Stephen, 102, 118n
Williams, James, 12, 21n
women, 3, 11, 33, 111, 115, 128, 136

Zeno, 150

DELEUZE AND GUATTARI STUDIES

A bold and genuinely interdisciplinary journal, *Deleuze and Guattari Studies* aims to challenge orthodoxies, encourage debate, invite controversy, seek new applications, propose new interpretations and above all make new connections between scholars and ideas.

Deleuze and Guattari Studies does not limit itself to any one field: it is neither a philosophy journal, nor a literature journal, nor a cultural studies journal, but all three and more.

www.euppublishing.com/dlgs

 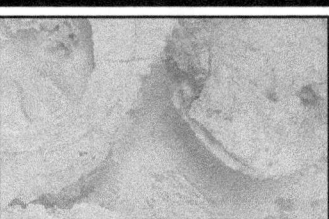 

Print ISSN: 2398-9777 | Online ISSN: 2398-9785

EDINBURGH University Press